# STAND

Emotionally and Practically Surviving
When a Child Gets a Life-Threatening Diagnosis

# STAND

Emotionally and Practically Surviving
When a Child Gets a Life-Threatening Diagnosis

JAY MITLO

*Stand: Emotionally and Practically Surviving When a Child Gets a Life-Threatening Diagnosis*

ISBN 979-8-9909003-4-9 *(paperback)*
979-8-9909003-5-6 *(e-book)*

Editing, formatting, and cover design services by
ChristianEditingandDesign.com.

# In Memory

Sean Patrick Boyle: "Meet you in Heaven, Buddy.
Love, Dad."
2/11/85–12/14/90

_____

Thaddeus Marquis Honor Gullett
1/23/13–10/11/23

_____

In loving memory of Sawyer Rebholz, who loved
Jesus and others deeply, smiled every day sweetly, and
filled the lives of his loved ones with so much joy.

_____

In loving memory of Nikki Deniker, who
continues to touch the lives of those still battling
through her Thinking of Nikki Foundation.

_____

In loving memory of Kate Dillon, whose faithful
love and trust in Jesus sustained her throughout her
battle until the Lord took her to His home.

# Tributes

Jayden Jaworowski: You are an amazing advocate for yourself and what you need. Every medical professional coming your way knows they have to address you first and tell you who they are, what their title is, what they're doing, and why they're doing it. You never cease to amaze with your self-advocacy skills. Whoever said nonverbal kids can't advocate for themselves has never met you.

———————

Josiah Jaworowski: You find joy in everything you do and are a one-man party! You are compassionate with others and love to make them smile with hugs, giggles, and dancing. Your smile and laughter are contagious, and I love how you want to share our flowers and also read stories about Jesus with others.

———————

Daniel J. Amato: We are grateful to the Lord for your healing.

———————

Sophie Stophel: We love your passion for wanting to make a difference in the oncology field.

# Thank You

I am very grateful for the Lord and His continual provision for me. He carried me through this entire process, both the battle and this book. What words could I use to properly thank Him? I would never want to go through any of this again, but I would never give up what I've learned about God and His love for me.

To my strong and faithful wife, Rachel—you are beyond incredible. We couldn't be more different in how we go about this grieving process, but you have supported me the entire way. You have sacrificed your comfort so that others could be blessed. You have always believed in my ability and encouraged me to follow my heart. When I met you, I stated that God's fingerprints were all over you. I have never been more right in my entire life. I love and thank you.

Joe and Bella, you are truly an inspiration. You are both much stronger than you would ever have imagined. You loved and supported Trey. You never resented the attention that he received. You refused to let his death crush you. You have never used what the enemy threw at you as a crutch or an excuse. You have dared to heal. You have had an impact on and encouraged more people than you will ever know. I love and thank you for who you are and how you've handled this life.

To my entire family—you were always there for us. There is such a stability in being a Mitlo. There's a guarantee that someone will always be fighting alongside you in their own way. You truly personify the body of Christ in that the parts make up a beautiful whole. Each of you used the gifts that God has blessed you with to help us through the most difficult part of our lives. I love and thank you.

To all of Team Mitlo - One, you did it. You helped us survive. You were there for us. You kept us from feeling alone. This book is possible because of you. Thank you.

Without the Center for Relational Care, I would have crashed and burned the moment Trey was diagnosed. You trained me and blessed me with the tools to navigate this battle.

Christian Editing and Design took a dream and made it a reality. You not only edited and designed my book but transformed the way I presented what I knew. Most of all, you joined me. You listened, grieved, and came alongside me in this process. I will forever be grateful for your giftedness and heart.

This project would have looked much different and the impact much less if my amazing niece Mia DeFazio did not take on the role of social media director. Your impact on me exceeded the incredible value of your work.

Anthony Barlich and Talia Nelson contributed to some of the pictures throughout the book. You selflessly blessed our family years ago and now are blessing many more. Thank you.

# Acknowledgements

We have been supported by so many people in various ways over the years. One significant way we have been supported over the past few months is financially helping me get this information from a Google Doc into an actual book.

Cori Tray, the Boothby family, Kelly Anker, the Brouzakis family, and Diane Milowicki all helped at the "Bronze Level" of contribution. They all represent different times and facets of my life. I am honored that they would help fund this project.

The Pleczkowski family, "Trey's Girlfriends" (a directed code from an otherwise anonymous person), Trey's actual cousins, and Jared Frank all contributed at the "Silver Level" of support. Without them, this would have been a far different process. They believed not only in helping others but in my ability to do so.

We had one anonymous person who was a "Gold Level" producer. Their exact quote was, "It's not about a thank you! If you could help someone else that has gone through what you've been through, then that's good enough for me."

Lastly, without Bill and Betty Ann Tis, this project would not have happened. Their generosity gave me the financial flexibility to even consider putting this book together.

To all of the folks listed (awkwardly) above, thank you. More than a financial contribution, you gave me encouragement, respect, confidence, and support. When people are blessed and they navigate the horrific waters of a child with a life-threatening diagnosis, you can know that you helped make it better . . . or less worse.

# Contents

# Author's Note

"Therefore put on the full armor of God,
so that when the day of evil comes, you
may be able to stand your ground, and after
you have done everything, to stand."

— Ephesians 6:13

I HAVE LIVED THE SAME LIFE ANYONE ELSE HAS. There have been ups and downs, mountaintops, and dumpster fires. I have been blessed, and yet I have sinned. In what I thought was a noble thing to do, I gave up my professional life to go into ministry. I found myself to be a bit of an outsider in both places. I was too Christian for the real world and too raw for the church crowd. All of that became just noise when I experienced the challenge of my life.

I struggled and was daunted by what was before me. Then, an extremely famous piece of Scripture came to me—the full armor of God. I had led a Vacation Bible School on it. I had read it many times and felt shame for not knowing it like the back of my hand. Now, something stood out for the very first time. I had read Ephesians 6:13 many times but had never really seen it—Stand. When the day of evil comes . . . Stand. I didn't need to conquer, win, or even advance. THAT . . . that is something I can do. I can Stand.

So that's what I built my ministry around, Standing alongside others so that they may Stand when the day of evil comes. I'm still not religious enough for the church crowd, but the people who need to see God's love are impacted by my love for them. It's love that makes a difference, and love means keeping people from feeling alone in their battles. After all, that's what Jesus did for us. He entered our world so that we would not be alone, forever. He came alongside us in a battle we could never win on our own.

That is why I wrote this book. I want to be able to Stand beside you. I want you to know that you are not alone. I want to equip those around you to best keep you from going at this all by yourself, and to certainly not make things worse (as Christians often do). I want you to be able to face whatever you are facing . . . and *Stand.*

# Foreword

O N CHRISTMAS EVE OF 2010, WE GOT THE WORST NEWS . . . the kind we never thought we'd get. "Cancer. Your son has cancer." Everything changed that day. We were going to become *those* people. You know . . . the ones with the poor bald kid. The ones that everyone looks at with such great pity and sadness. We were going to become the tired, tattered poster family for public sympathy. We could . . . become the family that loses a child.

That day began, or really continued, a journey that would dramatically change our lives forever. We would experience the greatest of victories, the sweetest that life has to offer, and the most devastating of lows and setbacks. We would never want to go through that again, but we also would not trade what we've learned in the process for anything.

If you or someone you love has received that same or similar news, this book is for you. We will share with you what we did, but also apply what we've learned to people who are different than we are. Not everyone has the same resources, family, community, diagnosis, or emotional makeup. However, *everyone* will have to make decisions along the way. Our hope, aim, and goal are that this book can act as a guide to making those decisions that will best get you or them through this.

Each chapter will tell our story, but then at the end will be two more sections. First, there is the "How To Stand" guide, which is aimed at the parents and immediate loved ones of the child who have received the diagnosis. Then, there is the "How To Help Them Stand" guide, and that is focused on all the people around them in their world. Other family, friends, church people, community members, and people who hear of their battle along the way are all included in this section.

Occasionally there are specific encouragements to types of people who tend to inadvertently cause the most harm while trying to help.

Above all else, know this . . . you can get through it. You can be a blessing to those in their battle. You can find beauty in the darkest of places. This horrific challenge doesn't have to ruin you, your family, or your loved ones. You can experience the worst life has to offer . . . and be okay. You can Stand.

# CHAPTER 1

# How We Got There

RACHEL AND I WERE MARRIED IN 1999. I had been on staff for a Christian youth outreach ministry (Young Life) since 1996. Rachel and I even met through Young Life; she was a volunteer leader in another part of Pittsburgh. Our marriage was good, even exemplary. In 2008, we were given the opportunity to go to the Center for Relational Care in Texas during my sabbatical from Young Life. What we learned there, and on subsequent trips, changed everything about our lives.

We learned what love can really look like. Love is more than an emotion. It is a choice. It can connect people and let them rejoice together and mourn together—like it says in Romans 12:15. We learned that love is the way to pull someone out of feeling *alone* with *comfort*. The reason why they feel alone is that their emotional needs are not being met. We learned how to join each other in our emotions. We learned how to rejoice with one another. We learned how to comfort. This teaching and understanding would drastically impact what we were about to face.

Our family was growing. Joe was born in 2003, Bella in 2005, and, finally, Trey in 2008. For some reason, I grew more and more hesitant to have another child. I feared we might have a child with special needs. Certainly, that wouldn't be the end of the world, but it would certainly be inconvenient. I was selfish, only thinking of myself and the impact any potential problems would have on my life. I was for sure being honest. Perhaps God was preparing me through those feelings of hesitancy. The fact that I was even considering . . . and fearing . . . possible outcomes was unusual. Regardless, all three were healthy, vibrant, spirited children. Until they weren't.

In the fall of 2010, Trey was playing on the floor and exclaimed, "STUCK!" He couldn't get up. For the next few days . . . and then weeks . . . he would say he was "stuck" and not be able to get up off the floor. He began to walk with a noticeable limp, and so we did what you do as parents. We took him to his doctor, who referred us to a few different specialists. We ended up at Children's Hospital of Pittsburgh (CHP).

I remember walking around the hospital with Trey. The poor kid was limping badly at that point. He would still play with the toys and look at the trains, but he was in pain. I carried him a lot. I remember looking at the various kids, especially the ones with bald heads, going by. I saw the beleaguered look on their parents' faces. During that time, I prayed. I didn't pray for us. I prayed for them. Those poor people. Can you imagine having a child with cancer? I asked God to be there for them, to give them strength, and to heal them. I remember feeling good about myself that I wasn't just there for my boy, but I was praying for theirs.

After several different specialists, we finally got a diagnosis. Trey had some rare autoimmune arthritis thingy (yeah, not the final diagnosis). It would come and go and could be treated with meds. I didn't like it, neither the diagnosis nor the feeling of having gotten it. I was uncomfortable with the uncertainty of it. However, it could have been much worse, so I was somewhat relieved.

Then, a few days later, the phone rang and we were told to come in the next day, as they had some more information. They wanted us to bring Trey back in to discuss what they had found. Following that phone call, I guess we didn't want to believe what was, looking back, pretty obvious to us now . . . this was not going to be good news. I remember saying, "I'm okay with whatever they have to say, but it better not be cancer." The person I was with warned me not to make such declarative statements. This, by the way, is not helpful, nor is it good comfort to share with people facing unknown, potentially bad news about their child. I would have much rather been joined in my emotions and not told how to feel about or approach the coming day.

So, there we were, Christmas Eve of 2010, when Rachel, Trey, and I went into CHP. Joe and Bella were . . . somewhere . . . maybe at my mother's? Soon, caring for Joe and Bella would go to another level. As it was, at this point we were ushered up to the top floor. We noticed the kids' beds that looked like cages with bars that went all the way up. *These poor kids!* I thought as I passed room after room, still in some sort of denial. We got into our room, and Dr. Shaw walked in. He said lots of words I will never remember. He ended it with, "Trey has neuroblastoma."

After an awkward pause, I asked, "What's that?"

"Cancer," he said. "Your son has cancer."

My first reaction, my first horrific thought, was, *I may lose my son.* He explained everything we would be facing in the coming days, weeks, and months. My second thought was (selfishly, but honestly), *This is going to be a lot of doing.* Everything had changed.

## How To Stand

When something is wrong with your kids, you don't know what you don't know. Overly simple? Sure. However, worrying and wondering doesn't help anyone. Take note of things in your life. What burdens your heart? Is God trying to tell you something? Some things always make much better sense in hindsight, but maybe you've missed something. If you have someone you can completely trust, talk with them. If they can give you input without judgment, and they really know your heart, God can and may speak through them. However, if it's someone who isn't going to take who you are into consideration and who would instead try to "flex" their knowledge or opinions, I'd encourage you to avoid that unnecessary complication.

Then, do your due diligence. Go to the doctors. Get your information. Grow what you know. More on this later, but DO NOT become your own doctor and devour everything on the internet. Allow the specialists to be the experts in diagnosis. Do they make mistakes? Sure. They even diagnosed Trey incorrectly for a few days. You have to deal with what is before you, and you need to not be encumbered by what might be. Whatever it is will be plenty enough without adding additional complications that *might* occur based on the depths of the internet or the unsolicited (or even solicited) advice of others.

If you haven't had a long run-up to your child's diagnosis, you are most likely . . . overwhelmed. Of course you are. Take hold of that which you can truly rely upon. Do you have family, friends, or neighbors who can keep you grounded at this moment? Lean on them. Take someone with you (if possible) to the doctors. Many hospitals have patient advocates or social workers who may be able to help you. That extra person will be able to hear things you cannot. Do all you can to not be alone as the news unfolds.

If you are walking alongside someone who is going through something like this, don't feel the need to prepare or warn them. It is not your job to prepare them for what might be ahead. You can't. Simply join them in whatever they're feeling. Do not allow them to feel alone, guilty, or ashamed of what they're going through. Feel it with them. They will remember you joining them forever. If you try to fix them, focus them, prepare them, or warn them, they will remember that too, but not in a good way.

# How To Help Them Stand

Pray. It is said more than it is done. However, really pray. Also, be praying much more than telling them you are praying. They know that people are praying. When you tell them you are praying, it almost seems like it's for you and not them. It's as if you don't know what to say, so you tell them you are praying. They will get a lot of that.

After that, judge your relationship with those who are directly in the battle. How close are you? Should you be *in* the battle? If you are sure you are where you should be—gently on the outside—even then, still tread carefully.

Don't assume you have priority in any way. They shouldn't have to return your phone calls, answer your texts, acknowledge your contributions, etc. A former volunteer leader with Young Life (who had quit years ago and burned a lot of bridges on the way out) texted me out of the blue when she heard about Trey (one year in) and asked me to call her about it. Did she realize how many people were ahead of her who I wasn't able to call?

Also, do not give assurances that are simply not guaranteed. I will always remember a member of our community telling me shortly after Trey was diagnosed, "Don't worry; my friend's son had neuroblastoma. He's fine now." It seemed so dismissive. It was as if *she* didn't want to worry, so she was telling me not to worry. Sorry, I was going to have to take this seriously. If she knew how many times I revisited that statement over the years, I'm sure (or I would hope) she never would have said it.

Realize that for those in the battle who are not the immediate parents of the child, this is still a very scary and overwhelming experience. You can do a lot of good coming alongside and supporting them through this time. This is terrible for them, as they are consumed with helping their loved one in the battle of their lives while also being concerned for the child. Perhaps even read each "How To Stand" section and apply it to helping the ones who are directly helping the parents.

To those who are quick to comfort through words and catchphrases:

DO NOT SAY:

- "God has a plan"—He does, but now is not the time to say it.

- "They'll be fine"—you don't know that.

- "This will draw you closer to Christ"—it might; it might not.

- "I know so and so who went through this"—this is their child, their pain, their trial, and no one else's. If that kid made it, it doesn't mean theirs will and vice versa.

- "I know how you feel"—never say that. You don't.

# CHAPTER 2

# Clarity in the Chaos

WE CAME HOME FROM THE HOSPITAL AFTER BEING THERE FOR THIRTEEN HOURS ON CHRISTMAS EVE. We'd been texting with my family (very large, supportive, and involved). We walked into my mother's apartment, and everyone was amped up. They were all excited to see us and engage with Trey. I remember thinking, *Oh, this is how we're going to do this?* It was a hyper, nervous atmosphere. I got it. No one . . . NO ONE knew what to do. We were going to have to move on and have Christmas Eve. Joe, Bella, and certainly Trey had no clue what was going on and we could not tell them, not now.

We had a decision to make. Do we keep this private and close to the vest or put it out there? A very difficult and perhaps revealing question came to me. *What would bring God more glory, if Trey is healed or if he dies and we stay strong in our faith?* Either way, we knew we had to go public. We needed the prayers, love, and support that everyone would offer. Also, whatever happened, I knew it would be a great opportunity to be used by God.

We started the "Pray for Trey" Facebook page and watched the comments roll in. We were overwhelmed even though we'd expected it to some degree. By the time we got home, I received a message from a childhood friend who stopped by to drop off Christmas gifts for our kids. He said he just had to do something. I have come to realize this compulsion to *do* something is true of many people around those who are suffering. I remember feeling both blessed and burdened by his gifts. We, his parents and extended family, had only found out Trey had cancer a few hours earlier. Here was a somewhat distant friend who had decided to give us gifts that were for HIS kids. I was moved and impacted.

As we got ready for what would lie ahead, I began to pray. I thought, *How will we manage this? How do we go about it?* I believe that God blessed me with clear thinking . . . and a plan. Rachel would be on point for Trey's care. There's no way she wouldn't be. I would make sure Rachel would be okay. Further, I would make sure Joe and Bella would have three things taken care of:

1. They would have food, water, and shelter—the basic necessities.

2. They would live their lives as normally as possible. They could not get swallowed by Trey's disease.

3. They would be informed and prepared for what they could handle within the scope of what would and may lie ahead.

This simple plan helped us tremendously. Rachel was able to focus on Trey, knowing that Joe and Bella were okay (as okay as they could be). I was busy and spread out (much more my strength) and yet focused. We had a plan.

We then had to go to the hospital a few days later to have Trey's permanent IV line (Broviac) surgically implanted. We checked into the hospital and went up to floor nine, where they have really nice artwork of famous athletes who have visited and cared for the "cancer kids" there. We got into our room, and there it was, a bed-crib with a cage. It made more sense now: you can't have kids with IV and medicine lines jumping out of bed. Still, seeing your two-year-old behind bars . . . AND HAVING CANCER?!?! Too much.

It was then that I got a phone call. A pastor I had been working with told me he was coming down to CHP to visit us. Rachel and I spoke and decided we didn't want visitors. We were there to do work, to get through it, to battle . . . together . . . alongside and on behalf of Trey. We would reach out for and accept help outside of the hospital, but inside . . . no. This was our battle to face. I thanked him and told him we did not want him (or anyone) to come. Shortly after that, he called me from the lobby asking for the security code to come to our floor. I reminded him that we told him not to come, did not give him the security code, and sent him away. He was trying to be there for Trey . . . for us . . . because he felt it was what he was supposed to do as a pastor, but he didn't listen to us. I often struggle with guilt, but I did not feel guilty telling him to go.

We were in the process of figuring things out. There were things we could control and things well outside of our control, to say the least. We knew we had each other and a bunch of people who were with us. However, just because they were with us didn't mean they were our priority. We . . . Rachel, Joe, Bella, Trey, and myself . . . were the priority. Decisions we would make would have to begin there. If *we* were okay, we could then focus on how God was using this situation and us to bless others. However, if *we* weren't okay, we wouldn't be able to make it and certainly would be of no use to others.

## How To Stand

Early on, it's essential to figure out how you are going to battle this disease and survive this daunting challenge. Are you going to bunker down and go it alone? Are you going to reach out to your friends and family and have them serve as a buffer to the rest of the world? Are you going to go all in and let anyone help who wants to? Each of these has its pros and cons; it depends on who you are and what your emotional needs are. I would say that the worst thing you can do is not make a choice, as you will be adding another variable to a life that just got so much less certain. When you make a decision, you can then filter everything that comes your way through that commitment. Is this choice in front of you right now consistent with your decision? Does it fit with your overall plan, or are you acquiescing to others' wants or needs? You and your family are the priority. If you ever have the right to be selfish, it's now. If having others around and involved brings you life and peace, go for it. If you need minimal noise and variables, shut it down. Either way, have a plan, and make a choice. If the time comes and you need to switch the way you handle things, by all means, do so. However, don't make changes because others have imposed that upon you. Remember, you and your (immediate) family take priority.

## How To Help Them Stand

What they need now is affirmation, not advice. They are making decisions they never thought they'd have to make. If they haven't made up their minds yet on how to go about all of this, affirm that. Really focus on what they are feeling (as much as this is possible) and join them in that. Saying things like, "My head is spinning just thinking about what you're going through" or "This IS so hard. You're doing a great job just hanging in there" will go a long way toward giving them some peace.

When you give them (unsolicited) advice, it may come across that you disapprove of how they are handling things. Even if you don't approve, it's not your place to say it, and it likely won't be received constructively. They are swimming in emotional mud. It's hard for them to even breathe. They most likely feel quite victimized by life and circumstances. Try to see that they do not have the clarity of thought that you do, as you have the luxury of being on the outside looking in. Further, you don't have the full emotional picture they are dealing with. It is best, in these times, to affirm and support them. That's all.

# For Those Who Have Been Through Something Like This

Be mindful that those family members struggling before you . . . are not you. While you can be vital to their ability to make it through this struggle, realize that they may very well be different from you. Allow them to be who they are and to do what makes them comfortable. If they ask you for your opinion, feel free to gently give it. DO NOT barge in and take control. It will leave them feeling hurt and you feeling frustrated.

# CHAPTER 3

# God Is There

IN THE MIDST OF THE CHAOS, I BEGAN TO NOTICE SOMETHING. God was present, but in the most subtle of ways. I could say I was looking for Him, but I wasn't. He just appeared. No, it wasn't in an image on a taco or a smudge on the window. He appeared and cared for us through different people, both those near to us and those we didn't even know.

The day Trey was diagnosed and after Dr. Shaw had gone over all the information, we realized we hadn't eaten a thing in hours. I left Trey and Rachel up in the room and went down to the cafeteria. I stood before some random cook and tried to order, but no words came out. Instead, tears welled up in my eyes, and I just stood there, broken. I tried to speak again, but nothing came out. I was about to break down in front of a whole lot of people. The cook looked at me with greater compassion than I had ever received before (at least in a cafeteria) and simply said, "It's okay, man; take your time." This was not a social worker, therapist, or clergy member. He was just a guy seeing another guy who was dealing with the worst news he'd received to date. If people can be influenced by evil, then I most certainly believe that God's Holy Spirit can also take over a man in a given moment to provide whatever is needed (for the record, I believe both to be true). I was so very grateful for that man and God's love through him in that moment.

A few days later, on the first night of our first stay in the hospital, I tucked Rachel and Trey in for the night and went to my mom's to pick up Joe and Bella. There I found out that Joe had thrown up. Figuring it to be only nerves for all the chaos our family had been experiencing, we still planned for an 8:00 a.m. drop-off the next morning so I could be there for Trey's surgery. Shortly after we got home, though, Joe got sick again. As I was coming back upstairs from putting his sheets and pajamas in the washer, I saw Bella standing at the top of the steps (a rare thing past bedtime). Sure enough, she had tried to make it to the bathroom but had gotten sick all over the hallway on the way there. I now had two kids with a stomach bug, one with cancer facing surgery the next day, a mother who I now could not allow to babysit . . . and vomit all over the rug. I was cleaning the carpet with all these variables in my head when a thought came to me: *When you say, "I do," you have no idea what you're saying "I do" to.* I will have to expand on this when I write my book on marriage, but for now, you get the point.

I had to scramble to find someone to watch Joe and Bella. For various reasons, no one around here could. To be fair, it's a tough sell to ask people to share a stomach bug. I was frustrated, overwhelmed, angry . . . and sad. And I don't mean that I was feeling any of these feelings because of anyone; it was just at what I was having to deal with. I then got a text message from my sister Cathy, who lives four hours away. It was a picture of all kinds of vitamins and preventative medicines she had gathered to bring . . . and she was on her way! I wept. I just needed that someone, that small respite, that support, that small victory. I didn't begrudge anyone else who couldn't help us but was elated that she came through.

God had begun to show up through subtle moments when we were at our lowest. It was then that I remembered something from my training at the Center for Relational Care. Grief without comfort is pointless. It's just pain. I can't say I knew what was going on, but it started to enter my mind. God continued to reveal this to me on two more occasions.

One day during Trey's first stay in the hospital, I stopped at home for a quick shower before heading back. Everything hit me all at once and I started to weep. Joe and Bella were somewhere else, and I was alone. I thought to myself, *Oh no, I'm all alone! This is just grief and there's no one to comfort me!* I wasn't devastated, but what I'd been taught was in the forefront of my mind. As I got out of the shower, I heard the doorbell ring, so I threw on some jeans and headed downstairs. There stood my friend Dustin. Dustin and I were friends who had been closer in the past than in the present, but we were certainly still friends even if we hadn't talked in a while. He stood outside my front door and said, "I didn't know what to do, so I just came here." I collapsed into his arms . . . shirtless in jeans, no shoes, wet hair, no shame (certainly awkward, but no shame). I wasn't alone. As a side note, Dustin had gone through a devastating loss of his own earlier in his life. His brother had come to him then and said just what Dustin said to me. The Bible says in 2 Corinthians 1:3–5 that we comfort others with the comfort that we have first received. This principle was so very evident at this moment, and it was something I would use moving forward throughout my life and in my ministry.

On yet another night, early in our journey, I was alone again and sitting at the computer. I don't even know what I was doing or where everyone else was at the moment. For whatever reason, I started watching Chris Tomlin singing "How Great Is Our God." Tears started to flow. It was very late, and no one was coming over to comfort me this time. I actually thought, *Well, God, now what are You going to do? I'm all alone in my grief.* At that very moment, I got a private message through a social media app. It was from some missionary in India named Amol who had heard about our family and Trey's struggle through a mutual friend. His message? He said, "Shalom," meaning peace. God sent me peace from thousands of miles away through someone I'd never met before. My tears of sadness turned to tears of joy that God was intimately aware of how I felt and knew exactly what I needed. Amol and I are friends to this day, and God has always used him to be there for me.

God was there and provided for us time and again. Is it okay to be mad at God? Many books have been written about that subject, and there is great evidence of others being angry toward God in the Bible, in particular throughout the Psalms. My brother has told me that just because it's in the Bible doesn't mean it's a good idea. I tend to agree. I just find it to be less than pragmatic. I've never thought I'd win an argument with Him, and I believe that it would only delay what I was to learn about Him. If it draws you closer to Him, then I suppose it's not in vain, but I simply chose to trust His ways and not my own. That proved to be what was best for us moving forward. Without that trust, I don't know what our lives would have looked like.

# How To Stand

What you are going through is an incredibly difficult time, to say the least. Very often, we want to look for a way to blame something or someone for what is going on in our lives. It's only natural. When something like this happens, evil rejoices. The enemy delights in despair and confusion. We can choose to seek God, His people, His love, His comfort, His provision, and His peace, or we can lash out at Him. Your other option is to leave Him out of this entirely.

If you are going through this, let's call it what it is . . . an attack. I would simply encourage you to be still. Be as still as possible and be aware that these circumstances, this diagnosis, this attack on your child and your family is as much a spiritual battle as it is physical. Know that God is not unaware of what you're going through. He is nearer than you think. If you can look for Him, you will find Him. If you can't, it's okay; He's still there. You can try to go it alone, for sure. You can try to just leave Him out of it. I will tell you this, that it's better with Him in so many ways.

## How To Help Them Stand

This is a spiritual battle. Not only is a precious little (or big) life on the line, but so are relationships with Christ. It will break your heart to see people angry at God. It will possibly frustrate you that they are turning from the very One who will see them through this. It may just feel as if there is no hope at all. Rather than panic and talk to them, or, even worse, talk *about* them, why not go to God in prayer? Organize a prayer vigil at your church. Start a prayer chain. Get their names on other prayer chains across the country or the world. I had no idea and couldn't begin to count the number of people who were praying for us. It did, however, give me great comfort knowing that people were praying. On the contrary, if someone had come up to me to tell me I was NOT following the Lord in the right way at that time, I can't imagine the damage that would have caused to our relationship.

## For Those Who Feel the Need To Protect God (and Their Relationship with Him) in This

This will probably be very challenging, but I encourage you to pray more and say less. You don't need to be God's public relations manager. If they're angry, let them be angry. If they are sad, let them be sad. When Jesus saw Mary and Martha weeping because He hadn't (yet) healed their brother Lazarus, look at both what He didn't do and what He did do (John 11:1–45). He didn't defend Himself. He didn't explain what was about to happen. He didn't shame them for their lack of faith. He joined them in their emotion and wept with them.

When "the day of evil comes," the enemy is trying to divide. In our case, he was trying to take our son. He was trying to separate us from God. He was giving us every opportunity to make ourselves bitter toward the doctors, our family, and anyone in our lives. It was only God who gave us the wisdom to seek Him throughout the entire battle. As we sought Him out, we found Him time and again. Don't allow the enemy to divide you from the very people who need your support and love. In the same way, don't allow the enemy to use you in a scheme to separate them from God, regardless of your intention. Trust that God *is* in control.

# CHAPTER 4

# Friend or Foe?

EVERYTHING HAPPENS SO FAST. You can go from a vague inclination that something's wrong to a doctor announcing, "Your child has cancer" quickly. In no time at all, you can have already been to the hospital several times and had some procedures take place. It wasn't for months, if not years, that I had a revelation about what we instinctively did that many families miss.

I had spent the first twelve years of my professional ministry career working for Young Life, where I focused on personally, and as a team, building relationships with high school students. We did this by building relationships with volunteer leaders, building relationships with people in the community, and building relationships with the schools and churches. You probably realize that we were all about building relationships.

It was in that relational manner that we treated our primary doctor, Dr. Shaw, and the staff of Children's Hospital of Pittsburgh. From the beginning, we were open, honest, and vulnerable. We put our trust in him and the whole team. Dr. Shaw told us at one of our first meetings to do our very best to let them be experts, for us to exclusively focus on Trey, and if at all possible, not to start searching "neuroblastoma" on WebMD. We never searched it—not even once. Instead, we began a great relationship with Dr. Shaw. He got to know us, and we got to know him. I could get him talking about rugby, music, food . . . whatever topics that made him another person on the planet rather than only the serious doctor we had trusted with our son's life.

One day on our third or fourth round of chemo, we were told that it would be a three-day stay. On day two, I mentioned to the doctor on duty (not Dr. Shaw . . . one I didn't particularly mesh well with) that we would be leaving the next day. She explained that we were there for three more days. I reminded her that we were told three total. "Well, you got here Monday, then there's three days, and so you leave Friday," was her response. I nearly lost it. I had to go back in the room and tell Rachel that we . . . that she and Trey . . . were stuck there for two more days than we had planned to be. I knew she wasn't going to be happy. I was not happy.

Rather than going on a rant on social media or demanding to speak with a superior, I reached out to my brother, Tom (who had worked with the healthcare industry for years). I didn't need to make things worse or have a bunch of people telling me how they had similar experiences when this or that happened to them. I needed someone I knew, and who knew me, to be there for me in that moment. What he said shocked me.

At one point in our conversation, he said, "Well, they probably need to fill a bed. Sometimes if there's a gray area and beds are open, it makes financial sense for the hospital to keep someone there." Mind you, he didn't say that is what they were doing for certain . . . he just said it could be. This blew my mind! I nearly flipped out. How dare they? How could they? Here I was, trusting them like a chump, and now my wife and son were stuck here for days. Righteous indignation? Full of it. Helpful? Not so much.

I then carried it a little further in my head. I wished that on Day One, I would have had the most curmudgeonly guy from my church put on a suit, carry a legal pad, and introduce himself as my family attorney who I had on retainer . . . who would be documenting everything that was said. I'll bet if I had done that, we wouldn't be staying here for an extra two days!

Except, maybe we would. Also, if we had come in all lawyered up, or even just thinking about being so protected, we would have been adversarial in all our conversations with the doctors, and they would have felt like they were on pins and needles around us too. The amount of emotional energy that being adversarial would have taken from us would have been very necessary energy . . . elsewhere. That's just not who we are. Would we have received better care? Would we have been checked in and out any faster? Would we have had a special flag on our account that would have gotten us treated with kid gloves? Maybe, probably not, but that point is moot. We never would have survived emotionally if we'd spent all our time and limited energy battling those who were trying to help us.

Very late in Trey's treatment, after both chemo and surgery (more on that later) had failed, we asked Dr. Shaw about some experimental therapy we heard might be available in Texas. We asked if it was something we should pursue. His response was, "If there was something on the moon that could save Baby Trey, I would take him there myself. What they're doing down there won't help him, and, in fact, is cruel." Did you notice what he said? "Baby Trey." Trey was six years old at this point. Dr. Shaw truly, deeply cared for Trey. He cared for us all. Would we have had the same response if we had gone at him from Day One? Professionally, any health care provider will tell you yes, but the reality is that people treat people the way they are treated themselves . . . at some subconscious level at least. I don't think for a second that Dr. Shaw, or any doctor, would ever do less than their very best. I am saying that sometimes it's better to have someone personally and professionally invested in what they do. If that opinion is wrong, I do know it's what was best for us. The fact that we had a good relationship with him and the other doctors resonated with our values. That's why we decided to build relationships with the staff as if they were real people and not just medical functions for our child's health.

# How To Stand

There is going to be a relationship between you and the hospital and doctors. How that relationship is going to go is primarily up to you. If you make up your mind early as to what type of relationship you're going to have, it will help avoid a lot of hurt feelings down the road. Are these trained medical professionals with you, or are they merely part of a necessary evil that you must endure? Can they help you emotionally as well as medically, or are they to be employed only as medical experts (hopefully) but kept at arm's length at all times? Basically, it comes down to this: do we treat them as friends or foes? I can't say that our being nice didn't cause us to be taken advantage of once or twice. I also can't say that it did. I can't say that we wouldn't have had quicker communication (the squeaky wheel gets the oil) or other benefits if we had been more adversarial. I don't know that we would have, either. I do know that it is best to know *how* you're going to relate to the professionals caring for your child and stay consistent with that approach. There are plenty of other variables in these times, so try not to let one be that you keep switching your attitude and emotional energy back and forth with the staff.

Dr. Shaw was exactly who we needed. When we looked into getting a second opinion after Trey's diagnosis, everyone told us to check with him, as he was the local leader in pediatric cancer. So, not only was he well respected in his field, but he was great with us as parents. Not all doctors are Dr. Shaw. Many are completely (or seemingly) detached from their patients. When all the doctors get together to brainstorm for the care of their patients, they call it "the tumor board." How gross is that? I suppose it's better than calling it the "if we screw up, a child dies board," but there must be something in between. I didn't want my child's doctor weeping and crying every day, but I didn't want robots, either. Dr. Shaw clearly cared for Trey and for us. I will take that every time.

## How To Help Them Stand

Remember that you are not them. Try to imagine just how much time they are going to be spending in that hospital in the coming weeks or months . . . even years. This will become a very sad second home for them. However they choose to interact with the hospital will be a matter of survival. As with everything in this process, it is vital to realize that they are not you and you are not in their shoes.

What they need in this time is . . . whatever they ask for. They may need a word of encouragement, a meal, parking vouchers, gifts, tasks done at home . . . it could be anything. Find out from somebody in the battle with them what they need and supply it.

## If You Consider Yourself To Be a Hospital Expert

Choose your words wisely. This hospital may not be like the one where you had your experience. Perhaps you did experience incompetency and had to advocate for your loved one on a continual basis. That doesn't mean that this hospital will be inept or that these parents have the same emotional makeup that you did then. I would argue that how this family you are trying to support interacts with the medical professionals on their team has much more to do with who *they* are than who the professionals are. You can neither make a passive person become a fighter nor make a facts-only type of person

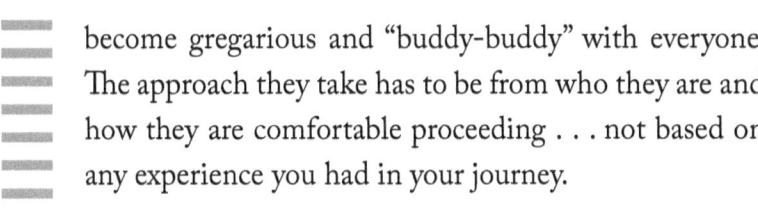

become gregarious and "buddy-buddy" with everyone. The approach they take has to be from who they are and how they are comfortable proceeding . . . not based on any experience you had in your journey.

CHAPTER 5

# Team Mitlo - One

G ETTING THROUGH THIS WAS GOING TO BE (AND ALREADY WAS) A LOT TO TAKE ON AS A FAMILY. We also quickly came to the realization that our experience was impacting people far beyond our nuclear family. On that first extended visit to the hospital, we got word that many people were wanting to help. Two women in our community who we were friendly with, but not really close to, started ordering wristbands for us. You know, the stretchy silicone ones that always have a quippy phrase in support of someone in their battle? *I guess that's just what you do,* I thought to myself. As I mentioned in chapter 2 about Joe and Bella not getting swallowed up by Trey's disease, I didn't want even the wristbands to be centered *entirely* around Trey. So instead of "Young Warrior," I came up with "Team Mitlo - One." It was about all of us.

Other friends and family read or heard that infection is a very dangerous threat to a child (or anyone) undergoing cancer treatments. They wanted to clean our home from top to bottom before we returned. Dr. Shaw pointed out that there was no need to go overboard, but that it might do everyone some good to be able to help in some way. That stuck with me. So, the weekend before we came home, there were over twenty people in our home cleaning everything you could possibly imagine. Even writing this now, I can't believe that Rachel was okay with this strange but oddly positive invasion of our privacy, but that goes to show you how much shock we were in. Rachel's fifty-year-old Young Life leader (from when she was in high school) was cleaning the microwave vent in the kitchen next to our thirteen-year-old nephew. Neighbors were cleaning next to people from our church. A real sense of community and "family" was developing beyond wearing a wristband. There were people ready to get dirty to help us out. For Rachel and myself, the support was palpable and comforting.

I asked myself, "If we truly are Team Mitlo - One, what about Joe and Bella?" At this point in their lives, they were just normal, everyday kids. They went to school, hung out with friends, and enjoyed their family. However, things had changed. I'm not sure exactly when, but at some point, we had to tell them about Trey having cancer. Joe was seven at the time and Bella was five. What could they understand? What could they handle? One day we went for a walk with them (I don't know where Trey was or what he was doing) and said, "Trey is in a race. He's in a race against a disease called cancer. We're all in this race with him. On our side, we have everyone in our family, tons of people praying for us, and the best doctors in the world. However, if we lose the race, which could happen, Trey will get to be with Jesus in heaven. Either way, Trey will win, but we could lose him. We are going to do everything we can to win. Beyond that, you guys need to know that you're going to be okay." They took it as well as any kids their ages could have.

However, how could Rachel and I make sure that they were okay? Making sure meant making a plan for each of them. We needed to be intentional in providing for them emotionally . . . and in every other way as well. Rachel and I knew that they needed a life outside of this turmoil. They needed people who cared about them first, and us second. We immediately enrolled Joe in jiu-jitsu. Was that a passion of his? He didn't even know what it was when we signed him up. We just wanted him to have a positive physical outlet for the frustrations that would be coming his way. We did not realize we were expanding our world to include an amazing team of people who never would have known about our situation. The men and women of Stout Training became an essential part of Joe's life for the next seven years. He never loved jiu-jitsu, but he did know that the people there loved him. While we hoped it would help, none of us knew how much it really mattered that he had a life outside of his brother's cancer.

Bella was (and still is) my sassy princess. She was sweet and snarky. She was kind and fierce. She was already the middle child, and all that the term has come to mean for so many families with more than two kids. What impact would all of this have on her? Two women in particular played an instrumental role in coming alongside her. Jane Marra would pick her up and take her to her own home to bake cookies. Alongside Jane's daughter, Christina, Bella would be the focal point of attention doing something, anything, that wasn't all about Trey or cancer related. It's incredible to me that Christina and Bella have a relationship to this day. Another dear friend, Becky Fenoglietto, would also take Bella under her wing from time to time. They would go out hunting for pixies (still not sure what that is), have breakfast or lunch, or just spend time together. These two women (and others I've failed to mention) stepped into the lives of a young girl needing to know that she was still special and deserving of love and attention.

In regard to Rachel, what could I do for a mom who was fighting for the very life of her son? I surrounded her with those who love her the most. For whatever reason, I set up a secret group of women who would bless and pray for Rachel. I guess I feared that Rachel would be embarrassed or feel like a burden if she knew who was sending her all these gifts or encouraging notes. It worked out wonderfully. Whether it was a Kindle to read during the stays in the hospital, her favorite type of wine (not red), gift cards, or sweet notes of encouragement and prayer, Rachel was moved. When we finally unveiled who they were, she was moved to tears—which is no small feat.

I made sure there were men in my life who had my back. My brother, Tom, was my go-to guy. I could call him 24/7 and he'd pick up. Another man always said to me, "Jay, when you can no longer Stand, I'll be kneeling in prayer beside you." I always knew that if things got really bad, I had those two men as an ace in my pocket.

"What about Trey?" you ask. When a child gets a life-threatening diagnosis, especially before they can even comprehend what that is, they become rock stars. Everyone wants to see them, bless them, and care for them at all times. One of the things Dr. Shaw told us to do was treat him like any other kid. He pointed out that many kids who survived cancer but were babied, coddled, or not parented became insufferable teenagers and adults. So, we continued to treat Trey like we did Joe and Bella. To do otherwise would cause developmental harm to both them and him. In regard to gifts, surprises, attention, and special trips, Trey would be receiving all that and much more.

These were the specific people who we already had in place to make sure we would all be as okay as we could be. *Many* other people had an immeasurable impact on our lives during those times. The Penn Hills community, the Penn Hills School District, the body of Christ, friends, coworkers, neighbors . . . together everybody became "Team Mitlo - One."

## How To Stand

Your immediate family must have all their needs met. Physical (food, water, shelter), intellectual (school, hobbies, activities), spiritual (faith, church, peace), and emotional needs (security, attention, support, affection, etc.) are all vital for you as you go through this kind of trauma. However, people will want to help and be there for you. These well-intentioned people can still be overwhelming. The key is to incorporate as much help as needed, not offered. Again, if you're ever going to be selfish, now is the time. It's about what is needed by you. You don't need to accept all the help that is offered. The more organized the help, the better. Again, have a plan in place to make sure that the family is served and the community is engaged. This helps everyone in the long run.

Dealing with everything that is going on while also coming up with a strategic plan for incorporating family, friends, and community to help you can be quite daunting. However, for some, working on a plan may give you a feeling of peace and control during a time when you have very little of either. If that organized person is not you, I'd encourage you to look around you. Is there someone who loves to plan and organize? If you trust them, have them do it. It could be your sibling, a member of your church, a coworker, or a neighbor.

However, maybe there isn't someone. If that's the case, I would encourage you to break the job up into manageable pieces. It might be just your immediate family. Someone needs to be in charge of food (meals). Another person or group of individuals should be assigned to each immediate member of the family to make sure you are all okay, or at least surviving. Anything above that is a bonus. You could have someone (neighbor, grandfather) make sure the grass is cut and the garbage is taken out (house-type stuff). Maybe there's someone who could take over doing the laundry. With each of these typically routine needs, if they give you life, then keep doing them. If they don't, and you can manage to do so, delegate them to others.

Lastly, what if you don't have a team? What if you don't have others? What if you don't have anyone? You might be new to the area or live a simple and private life. In that case, check with the hospital through their social workers to see what local organizations offer help. In Pittsburgh, there's a great organization called Pressing On. They are singularly focused on helping families in whatever way possible through these times. Beyond that, check with any group you are involved in. Boy or Girl Scouts, sports teams, social clubs, civic groups, and even your place of employment are all places to garner support during these times.

## How To Help Them Stand

This is another time (see chapter 1) where you can really step up and help the helpers. Help them by being the workers and labor for the projects that come up. Those who are leading the efforts to bless the immediate family need people to follow them. Make sure *their* needs are met as they directly come alongside the family.

Another way you can help is to spread the word about the battle this family is in. I was consistently amazed at how many people were aware of what we were going through and contributing in different ways—people who I didn't even know. Some of the more impactful help we received was from people we didn't originally know, but someone told them about us.

I mentioned in chapter 3 about not being God's PR department. When you spread the word, God uses *those* people to bless the family, and *that* has an impact on their faith.

CHAPTER 6

# Some Will, Some Won't

I MENTIONED THE TWO LADIES WHO ORGANIZED THE WRISTBANDS FOR TEAM MITLO - ONE. If you gave me one hundred guesses, I wouldn't have named those two as the first to step up. The man who dropped off the Christmas gifts the day Trey was diagnosed is a great, selfless friend . . . one I hadn't talked to that much in the previous year. He probably wouldn't have made my top fifty guesses as to who would do something like that for my family. Some people stepped up and we never saw it coming. There were many fundraisers organized by some of the most unlikely of heroes (more on that in the chapter on fundraisers). However, there were others who I would have guaranteed would be there for us. These were people whom we had known for years, friends we saw on a regular basis. Prior to Trey's diagnosis, we were very close. After his diagnosis? Either in short fashion or over the long haul, they were gone.

I will start with the positive. Our family was (and is) incredible. Immediately, they stepped up. The day Trey was diagnosed, we had a family Christmas Eve dinner at my mom's apartment. *What is THAT going to be like?*, I thought as I opened the door. Crazy, busy, nervous, loving, and loud is what we experienced as we walked in. Yep, that's our family. We were going to be as normal as we could be given the unprecedented news of the day. From that time on, each member of our family settled into their roles of love and support. My mother and father did what they could to continue to be who they were, loving grandparents who never thought they'd be dealt something like this in their lifetime, especially not to a grandchild. Know this: people like them (and all family to some degree) are grieving this twice. They are devastated by the news of their, in this case, grandson having cancer. They are also devastated at what's happening to their son or daughter. It just always struck me as a strange phenomenon. To some degree, I was only grieving once. You might think I would be thinking of, caring for, and grieving for everyone in this process. In all reality, I wasn't. That's who I am now. Who I was then was a father trying to hold his family together. With our entire family pitching in, our needs were met, and we did hold together. Rides, babysitting, phone calls, visits, *not* visiting, chores, whatever we needed, whenever we needed it . . . provided.

Our friends were incredible as well. Perhaps it was the fact that we had lived a very intentional life of building relationships with as many people as possible that blessed us with this resource. Again, each person did what he or she could do and was called to do to get us through it. Gifts, phone calls, fundraisers, distractions, time away from the disease, whatever it took and whatever was asked, they were there.

Our community, Penn Hills, gets a really bad rap. Once the shining suburb of the greater Pittsburgh area, we are not thought to be what we once were. You can take that idea somewhere else. From the schools, churches, and businesses to our neighbors and community members, we were lifted up and cared for beyond our imagination. Again, I should point out that we were already very involved in the community. I was a 1989 graduate of Penn Hills High School, and Rachel moved here in 1998. We ministered and cared for countless kids through the ministry of Young Life and coaching. That definitely benefited us during the Trey Days. Each of our kids was cared for by the teachers and staff of their respective schools. They were treated like normal students 99 percent of the time, but when they needed special attention or grace for a missed day or assignment, they got it. The teachers would check in but not obsess. It was always just enough but never too much. Fundraising events were well attended; we were never in want. At one point, we had let our insurance lapse, and I went into our state representative's office. He would not have known me from anyone else. However, I knew both ladies at the front desk, who both started crying when I walked in; they were clearly aware of our story. Within hours, $31,000 of bills (that occurred in three days) had been taken care of by them. I'm quite sure we had it better than most.

On the other hand, some disappointed us. To a degree, I suppose it's inevitable. I mean, you can't bat a thousand. There were folks who we thought would be there for us. There were those who we thought would have been spearheading the charge, taking us by the hand (not to be dramatic), and holding us by the hand. Well, in some cases, they let go. Most of the time, I found it to be confusing. One woman came up to me crying. I told her we were okay. "HOW CAN YOU BE?" she yelled at me. She pushed me away, and I never . . . ever heard from her again. Two others really disappointed me . . . one right away, the other after a while. As much as I can tell, it comes down to two reasons why people are not (especially the ones you thought would be) there for you.

1. They are reminded of and still hurting from a traumatic experience or loss in their own life.

2. It simply scares them. They cannot fathom what you are going through and can't bear to be around it.

I do know this. Their leaving, and their seeming rejection, was not a measure of their love for us. It was not intentional or mean-spirited. I'm sure they thought of it many times and felt terrible. Did it hurt then? Yes. Do I forgive them now? Absolutely.

# How To Stand

We were blessed to have so many people in our lives who wanted to and could help us. It constantly broke our hearts to see other parents (or single parents) not have the same resources that we did. You will need as much (organized) help as you can get. You (or someone) need to be prepared to manage people you don't even know, let alone the ones you barely know, but who want to help. It is important to incorporate people early on in the process to build momentum. If you (or whoever is organizing the volunteers) turn people away at the beginning, it is harder to get them back later.

At the other end are those who don't step up. It's just going to happen. As much as possible, try not to dwell on it. Realize that their distance is not about you (this is about the only thing in this time that isn't). It's about their story, their fear, their hurts. No one thinks, *Their child is in grave danger? Too bad for them; I have laundry to fold.*

Some people who you really thought would be there for you won't be. However, many, many more will step up to help you through this time. Take what you can get (and want).

## How To Help Them Stand

Similar to the last section, be mindful of those who have directly come alongside those in the battle. Extend grace to them when they don't have as much time for you as they have in the past. Don't be so quick to judge that they are "losing themselves" in their loved one's trauma. In regards to when people do not step up, you can be the voice of reason. Imagine this: the immediate family is let down when someone abandons them. Those surrounding them can be vital in keeping the pain from getting worse. They can also make it worse. Do your best to model *not* dwelling on those who have failed to show up. Encourage the helpers to help and not keep score against those who are not helping.

If you are not directly involved in helping them Stand, and others have let them down, maybe now is the time for you to step up. You could lead a fundraiser, mow their lawn, start a prayer chain or vigil, or whatever they need. Pray and then respond to how God leads you. Be gentle and humble, but if you feel led to do so, offer to be a blessing.

If you are someone on the periphery, be yourself. Feel free to communicate with those directly in the battle. Encourage them; affirm them; root them on. However, if the pain of what they are going through is too much for you, don't share that with them. Share that with another person outside of the battle. Those within have enough going on.

# CHAPTER 7

# Thank You ... I Guess

IN THE FIRST WEEK AFTER TREY WAS DIAGNOSED, SOMETHING HAPPENED (THE FIRST OF MANY) THAT WE DIDN'T EXPECT. Food, lots of it, came flowing in. I remember one night very early on coming home to several boxes and many bags of groceries and prepared food. I was exhausted from a long day at the hospital and then had to head over to my mom's to pick up Joe and Bella. Bath and bedtime, mail, phone calls, and texts . . . and then I had to figure out what to do with more food than we would eat in a week. Some of the food we would never eat. It took forty-five minutes to organize it and put it all away. I felt so guilty that I was upset about having to do this. All those who brought us food were nice enough to buy all of this, and I was feeling put out? Yes. I was feeling put out because close to an hour of work was added to my day when I had just about nothing left to give. Feeling guilty, I then made sure to give away what I knew we would never eat. Can you imagine agreeing to take food from a family battling cancer? It was not easy at all.

Very shortly after that, we started using a meal train app. It was great to have very clear and specific descriptions of what we loved to eat, wanted to eat, would never eat, and couldn't eat. We had someone (and I apologize to them for not remembering) agree to run this for us. Obviously, this was someone very organized and gifted in communication. When we needed to make changes to the original plan, and this happened often, the changes were taken care of for us. Instead of a daily decision or potential burden, it became a lot of fun for the whole family. The kids would ask who was bringing food over. Often whoever was bringing food over would stop in to either say hi or meet the kids (especially Trey, but the smart ones knew to fuss over all three kids). We certainly had our favorites, and yes, some really missed the mark. Gift cards were good too, but too many became a chore. Prepared food was the best and most appreciated by us.

I mentioned earlier that Rachel's ladies took really good care of her. It was important for me to make sure her needs were taken care of because she didn't have the time or mental energy to meet her own. On one of our first stays in the hospital, her CrossFit friends brought a computer into the hospital for us. We only had one laptop at the time and needed another one to watch videos and communicate via social media while in the hospital. We were moved, we were loved, and our needs were met.

It was vital that Joe and Bella did not feel left out. Granted, they didn't have cancer and they didn't have to go through treatments in the hospital. However, their brother was also getting a lot of attention and gifts. We actually set up a separate "meal" train for them. Rather than meals, it was gifts and special things just for them. Crayons, crafts, toys, and gift cards were delivered at least twice a week. More often than not, these "surprises" came in the mail (which was a bonus blessing . . . who gets mail anymore?), but occasionally it would be in person. This too was an added bonus with the surprise. They really looked forward to these diversions, and they really made a difference.

In the hospital, it was always nice to have meal cards for the cafeteria. It was just one last thing to have to deal with during our stays. Receiving cards and signs helped us decorate the room for each of our many visits. Very often the hospital would also have giveaways and special presents that had been donated to them. You can't ever keep it completely even for all the kids, and Joe and Bella would sometimes just have to realize that Trey was going through something big. Sometimes he got things that they didn't. Conversely, the hospital had something called the Sibling Center. This was a service specifically designed and created for the kids who weren't in treatment. We did not use this service as much as we had many other distractions and special things for Joe and Bella. When they did go, they enjoyed it but never asked to go. They preferred their attention to be given to them outside of the hospital.

People wanted to give, and I was more than happy to allow them to do so. I knew that it meant something to them to feel like, and know, that they were helpful and useful to our family.

I enjoyed seeing everyone be blessed by others. There are so few perks to having a kid with cancer. I would do my best not to let one slip by.

## How To Stand

Use a meal train app as soon as you can. Be very specific. Use exact companies if you are brand-specific. Do not be shy, and do not lie. People want to bless you, and bringing something you cannot or will not use is never their intention. Don't make them have to guess at your preferences. Have a drop box for when you are not home or can't (or don't want to) come to the door. Have a neighbor grab the food if the weather won't let it sit out long. It's also helpful to monitor and adjust the frequency of the meals when needed; this is more often than you might think would happen. You will need more food when everyone is home and less (and different) when there is a hospital stay.

Once again, if you have a friend who has committed to providing all of your meals and that gives you more peace than many different people dropping by all the time, then for sure, go with that. It's about meeting your needs first.

Make sure everyone in the family is getting something for them on a regular basis. The child who is sick will be showered with all kinds of gifts and attention. Make sure other siblings (and mom and dad) get some too. Don't be afraid to ask for this . . . and be specific. Don't rob someone of the opportunity to give as long as you don't look down on those who can't give as much as others.

It is very helpful to have a trusted loved one run each of these giving programs. It's just one less thing you have to run yourself. Whether it be someone you talk to regularly (family member, close friend) who keeps you from having to make another phone call or someone from the outside who needs a role, having that point person is extremely helpful. If, as always, this is a healthy distraction for you and you'd like to run it yourself, feel free! Remember, there are very few rules when it comes to this. You do what you can to survive and be the best (or, more realistically, the "least worst") version of yourself.

However, if you are someone who does not know a lot of people or is new to the community, this will look much different. I mentioned the Sibling Center in this chapter. There are other social services that can rally around and meet your needs during this time. Whether it be an organization like Pressing On or something that the hospital directly offers, find out and use any service that would be helpful. Finding organizations and services may be difficult on your own, but the hospital should know of and direct you to what is available. This may be a time to be more assertive than you are comfortable with. If that initiative pays off, it will be well worth it to help you with even one small aspect of your needs.

## How To Help Them Stand

I cannot begin to tell you how great it was when people dropped food off to us. On the one hand, it was a relief not to have to make sure the family had food to eat each and every night. However, there was another blessing that took time to realize. It was when more and more random people brought food over that I continued to see God working. Why did these people care about us when they didn't even know us? Why did they take such great care in preparing our meals when a gift card would have been fine? It was you, the people gently on the outside of this tragedy who dipped their toes into it, who reminded us that God was intimately involved in our battle.

With that being said, be careful not to overstay your welcome or make the drop-off about you. It's understandable that this is a socially and emotionally awkward moment for you. In some ways, the family is already getting used to the uncomfortable moments. You may be holding your breath and trying not to say something wrong. It's okay. Be yourself. Drop the food, gifts, or whatever off, say hi, read the room, and get out. Less is more, but none is lonely.

CHAPTER 8

# "My Hospital"

LATE IN TREY'S LIFE, WE WERE DRIVING DOWN ROUTE 28 TOWARD DOWNTOWN PITTSBURGH. Across the river and way up the hill in the distance was Children's Hospital. Trey looked over and said, "Is that my hospital?" Two things hit us at that moment. One, how could this boy know what the outside of "his" hospital looked like from a mile away? Two, he had said it was *his* hospital. Trey called it his hospital. That's how much time he had spent there. It wasn't just *the* hospital; it was *his*.

The reality is, that hospital had become all of ours. We never figured out how many nights Rachel (and Trey, obviously) had slept there. We certainly knew how many stays we endured and could count the number of surgeries, scans, and other procedures. We never would have imagined it would be as many nights as it turned out to be.

The hospital would give out beads to the children for each medical procedure they endured. They were color-coded for surgeries, blood draws, scans, and everything else. You were supposed to put them on a string and make a bracelet or necklace. Rachel and I would joke about how long Trey's was. She, like the mama bear she is, kept each and every one of them. As I sat down to write our story, I realized I had no idea what had happened to those beads. When I later checked with Rachel, I discovered that she's still got them and that she's brainstorming a cute art project to do with them. Those beads symbolized Trey's toughness. Wherever they end up on display, they will always remind us of our "Young Warrior" and the battles he fought.

I mention Rachel sleeping there as this was much more often the case than me staying overnight. This was our division of care. I was much more gifted at doing multiple things and being on the go. Rachel could and still can hunker down with the best of them. Given that Rachel was on point for Trey's care, it made sense for her to be the one with him.

We eventually set up a system and pattern for how to survive the hospital. Back in those days, internet access and screens weren't what they are now. We had to have a portable DVD player and a laptop, but even with these tools, we were still often at the mercy of the hospital's Wi-Fi. Videos, sadly, were a great way to pass the time. Having our toiletries, sleepwear, pillows, and small comforts from home didn't make it great but certainly made our experience less unbearable. We loved the signs and cards our support system made for us. When a gift was delivered, it helped too.

I loved having visitors. Rachel did not. When we had a stay in the hospital, Rachel went into bunker mode. She was going to do what she had to do to get through it. For me, I'd welcome anyone who would help me pass the time and distract Trey. I learned not to invite people to come when Rachel and I were both there . . . and certainly not if Rachel was alone. We had to do whatever we could to get through it for both Trey and us.

We had heard how other folks got to know other parents and children during their stays in the hospital. Some had formed lifelong relationships that started during similarly tragic times. That kind of outside connection was just not the case for us. It wasn't intentional. It just didn't happen. We were there because Trey needed to be there. Everything centered around that (and surviving it ourselves). As relational as we are, we had to be selfish, at least on some levels, in those times.

The only place we would ever see other parents was in the playroom. These places are incredible at CHP. There is one on every floor and a giant one on the sixth floor called Austin's Playhouse. I took any chance I could get to be with Trey in there. However, even the specially designed playgrounds at the hospital did present challenges. Trey had what he called his "crayons" that we had to protect all the time, at pretty much all costs. During his stays in the hospital, he would be hooked up to monitors and medicines through these colorful plastic ends of his permanent IV line. They did look like crayons, and so we all ended up calling them his "crayons." Basically, we had to drag an IV pole around wherever we went because that equipment carried with it whatever infusion or treatment he was on at the time. Imagine chasing a toddler around a busy playroom with a six-foot lead, and if that got extended too far, his cord would snap and we would have to rush off to get it reattached or even have surgery to fix it. The alternative to an IV pole, though, is that you stay in your room and do nothing but watch videos all day. The worst was when he was too sick or too susceptible to other germs that we couldn't go play and couldn't get out of the room at all. He knew about the playground. He knew it was right down the hall. Some days, he just couldn't go. Our son had cancer. Our son was sick. Our son was under horrific medicine . . . and we had to say no.

There is a lot of downtime in the hospital. Whether you're waiting to go down for a scan, waiting for a treatment, or just waiting, there is a lot of time in the room. Given that Trey was either getting lots of medicine or going through a lot of testing and scans, he was tired often and slept a good bit. That left time for us to get work done or time to read and surf the net (at least when the Wi-Fi would connect). For me, waiting left a lot of time to look out the window. Sometimes Trey and I did that together. I remember looking at people walking by in the street below. They were on their way to or from work. They were going to lunch. They were with other people. Many probably thought they were having bad days. I wanted so desperately to reach out and scream, "You have no idea what a bad day is!" If only someone had yelled that to me before Trey was diagnosed. Sadly, if they had, I, like those people on the street, would not have understood.

Understanding is something that many, if not most, of the staff at CHP have. The day we were told that Trey had cancer, we were obviously in shock. I mentioned the man in the cafeteria in chapter 3. I will always be grateful to and remember him. There were many more. "Sheriff Pete," our primary oncologist (AKA Dr. Shaw), showed understanding throughout. He knew that Trey would engage with him when he was silly and fun. He knew not to barge in with a quick knock. He *really* knew not to wake Rachel and definitely not to wake Trey (he learned the hard way . . . once). He knew that I liked to know everything and that Rachel liked to know only what she needed to know. The other oncologists on Trey's team were likewise adept at being human and treating us as people rather than just another case on their caseload.

The nurses were nothing short of a godsend. Sitting here now, I am trying to think if there were any that I didn't care for, and I am coming up blank. Having spent multiple nights on every floor of *his* hospital, Trey got to see, and we got to interact with, all the different nurses working within their specialties and callings. It was fascinating to see the ICU nurses care and dote on their one or two patients, while up on the ninth floor (oncology), they were more like DJs, constantly going from room to room, patient to patient, and meeting each of their needs. On the post-surgery or varied purpose floors, it was impressive to see their vast knowledge of our and the other kids' needs. Finally, the nurses in recovery post-operation knew how to get things done. Those individuals could get Trey ready to either go upstairs or go home, and they let us know exactly what was ahead of us. They each held a special place in our hearts, as they all treated not only Trey but us as parents with care as well. I will never forget Nurse Amanda standing next to me while I watched a Pittsburgh Penguins hockey game on TV as Trey slept (on one of *my* overnights). She had to go, as the hospital didn't like the nurses to spend too much time in one room. The game was in overtime, she wanted to see the game, and I was bored. I began to ask her questions about Trey's treatment of which I already knew the answers. That way she had to stay. Wouldn't you know it, just after the Penguins scored, I was done asking questions. Later, I found out that she was questioned by management as to why she was there for almost fifteen minutes. I was happy to confirm that she was indeed helping us through a trying time in those minutes. She got it. She loved Trey and cared for us all. They all did.

The front desk and check-in personnel were tremendous. They greeted us warmly and by name as they got to know us. They were never ingenuine in their attention or fake in any way. They could always read the room. When we were tired or Trey was fussy and not happy at all to be there, they were sympathetic. When I was being my normal, overtalkative self, they engaged. They knew why we were there. They knew we didn't want to be there. They treated us with respect and great understanding.

Yes, almost every person there treated us with great understanding and compassion. Sadly, not every one of them did. I remember a physician's assistant or maybe even a doctor (who wasn't one of Trey's primary doctors) in particular. This was the same one who told us that we had to stay for five days instead of three. She was always sharp and sarcastic. She would, to a degree, passively aggressively come at me like I was playing around. To be clear, and especially with her, I was never playing. I tried not to let it get to me or make it more than it was. However, any time she came into our room (which wasn't often), I would just get quiet. You can always know I'm not okay when I'm quiet. It was bothersome to me how bothered I got by her.

The residents . . . oh, the residents. I don't mean people who live somewhere . . . honestly, we felt like residents of CHP at times. No, I mean the new (right out of med school) doctors who would make rounds in the mornings and report back to the oncology team. Every morning they would quickly knock on the door and barge in just after knocking. What exactly did they think the knock accomplished? We never knew any of their names and they rotated around quite a bit. I would talk to Dr. Shaw and anybody else who would listen about it. It might get better for a day and then it would go right back to the same rude behavior. There were just some things you couldn't change.

If I had to encapsulate both the positives and negatives of our experience at "Trey's hospital" in one exchange, it would be this. There was a doctor who would oversee either Trey's stem cell transplant or immunotherapy (or both). He was highly regarded and apparently brilliant. He was also about as personable as a gas pump. Beyond that, he somehow failed to realize we didn't know as much as he did from a medical perspective. He would even get a bit frustrated when we would ask questions, but I suppose what he knew was more beneficial than his doctor-patient, or doctor-parent, behavior was detrimental. However, standing behind him each time he spoke with us was Jason. We called Jason "the Interpreter." The doctor spoke English just fine. It was just that the words he used were far above and beyond us, and outside of any semblance of our working vocabulary. Jason would calmly, warmly, and with great care explain to us what the doctor had just said. His job was to smooth over the bumps and dumb down the overwhelming, complicated information we had just received. It was a microcosm of our stays there. There was a necessary, uncomfortable reason for us being there, but there was also a thoughtful set of mechanisms in place to help us get through a tough time.

One of the few benefits of having a child with cancer, if it can really be called that, is that you get to call ahead and go to the front of the line (if you're not whisked in right away) in the emergency room. Infection is a huge risk for cancer kids when they are going through chemotherapy. Thus, sitting around a waiting room full of sick kids is dangerous. We had to go to the emergency room many times for a broken IV line (remember the "crayons") or when a fever would spike. It was always (obviously) unplanned and terribly inconvenient. The doctors there were not our primary doctors. They did not know Trey, nor was Trey at his best when he was there. They were never moved by my charm or wit and knew they wouldn't be seeing us for very long, even though it was always too long for us. These were the grind hours. We weren't there for treatment. We weren't advancing against cancer. These trips would often result in unplanned stays upstairs. It was just another terrible component of our lives at that time.

Due to his cancer, and to a degree the chemotherapy, Trey had to visit several specialists throughout the hospital. Whether it be physical or occupational therapy, hearing tests, vision exams, or the many, many MRIs, scans, and other treatments for neuroblastoma, he was expertly cared for and helped. I just can't imagine what our time there would have looked like if the staff hadn't handled themselves far and above what their technical expertise qualified them to do. They didn't just treat (or track) the cancer; they cared for our son.

Yes, it was Trey's hospital. It was ours as well. It was always a strange feeling walking down the hallway from the parking garage at the beginning of one of our stays, thinking, *We're back . . . this feels familiar.* We didn't want it to be familiar. We didn't want this to be our home away from home. However, everyone involved did a great job of making it another "least worst" experience in a horrific time.

## How To Stand

Nobody wants to be in the hospital. *No one* wants to be there for their child. Some of us, and you or your loved one, have to be there. You must do what it takes not to make it worse than it already is.

In regard to how things work, figure out who's going to spend the most time there and what their needs or likes are. Do you want food from home or takeout, or do you not mind the hospital food? Do you want visitors to help pass the time, or does that add to your stress? Do you want everything from your home in your room, or do you want to keep that space minimal and clean? Does it give you more peace to have help throughout the day and the stay, or does it make you feel better knowing that everything "on the outside" is being taken care of and you just have to be here handling things yourself?

It will help you to find out early on who you can trust completely. This goes back to chapter 3 and the idea of "Friend or Foe." You should have at least one doctor, one nurse, and one specialist that you can talk to and really trust; then you'll know you're getting the right information. If nothing else, it will help you get through the day.

Get familiar with the schedules of the doctors, interns, and specialists. Understanding how the hospital clock works will help you with your expectations in regard to service and expected waits. Realize that decisions typically don't get made during the weekend, as your regular doctors aren't usually there. If you don't get discharged by Friday, you're probably there until Monday. Sometimes you will get more candid answers to questions if you catch a weekend doctor (especially a semi-retired one) who isn't afraid to share what's going on. If your child is an inpatient, very often you will get bumped for emergencies and outpatient scans or services. With nap time looming, this can be infuriating. There's also very little you can do about it.

It will be up to you to overly communicate and question regarding how long your stay will be. Find out not only how many days your stay is expected to be but also what must happen before you can go home. What procedures need to take place? What is the recovery time? What markers does your child have to hit (temperature, weight, or other numbers) before it's safe to leave? The more you know ahead of time will give you fewer unpleasant extensions.

Sometimes the pharmacy at the hospital is its own world. We would be all ready to go home, but the meds wouldn't be ready yet. We would be packed, Trey would be spent, and we just wanted to go, but we'd have to wait. There's no trick or tip with this. Just be ready for it.

Lastly, remember that everyone there is doing their job. They have lives too. They are not only professionals or service staff but people as well. If you treat them simply for how they relate to you, what you receive will be very sterile. However, when it is possible, get to know them a little. Be a person to them, and you will become more of a person (rather than just a patient) to them. It will help.

## How To Help Them Stand

Children's hospitals all have different ways you can support a family that is spending time there. You can send e-cards, balloons, or flowers, just to name a few ideas. Most of it can be done in-house and not be delivered by anyone else. Further, you can pre-pay for meals or parking by gifting it to the family you designate. Again, these little acts of love from someone the family doesn't even really know make an impact over time.

Consider where you are gifted. Wherever those talents are, you can use them to bless not only the immediate family but also those who are in the battle with them. Maybe you give *them* parking passes. Maybe you make a meal for them as they are so busy caring for the family who's at the hospital. If someone's brother or sister is in the hospital with their child, perhaps you can pick *their* kids up after school or practice if you know them well. When people come together to care for a family in their battle, very often the helpers end up not meeting the needs of their own families. It may be your calling to be there for those who are helping. This can really be a good fit when you know the helpers better than you know the immediate family.

CHAPTER 9

# Fundraisers: More Than Money

RIGHT AFTER TREY WAS DIAGNOSED WITH CANCER, PEOPLE STARTED TO RAISE MONEY FOR US. They wanted to help us with medical bills, day-to-day finances, gifts for the kids, and whatever else was needed. I mentioned the wristbands early in chapter 5. When trying to figure out how much we should charge for those, the ladies pointed out that we had to charge enough to make money from it. That hadn't occurred to me at all. I had not even begun to think about raising money. Over the years, I have come to learn how important fundraising events are to us or any family in this kind of trauma.

There were so many fundraisers. "Dress down" days for the teachers from the schools where the kids attended, dances at Joe's school, an event full of baskets at a brewery, golf events, donations from nonprofits, online shops where we received the proceeds, a spaghetti dinner (I think those are mandatory), t-shirt sales, and more.

The first thing that impacted us in this whole process was the varied and (seemingly) random collection of people who organized these events. You would think (or at least I would) that it would be you or those closest to you who would initiate fundraisers. From the very beginning, I realized we would not be doing that. We had way too much going on, and just getting through the day was enough for us to handle. Also, we were struggling with all the attention we were receiving. We understood it, but it was still a lot. Clearly, I was more comfortable with it than Rachel, but even for me it was something more that I had to deal with and manage. For us to organize fundraising . . . for ourselves? That was just something we weren't comfortable doing.

In the same vein, those around us were consumed as well. Our family and friends were all stepping up to support us and get us through this initial wave of confusion and trauma. They had their roles in our lives and in this time. Fundraising was not one of those roles.

Early on, it was the schools that did the bulk of the fundraisers. Like I mentioned, there were multiple "dress down" days with the staff of the schools in our district. I was amazed at how much money would be handed over to us each time, overwhelmed by the generosity of our community. I was also moved by the kind words of those who sent notes and well wishes. With each event and each note, it was a greater and greater reminder that this wasn't a dream. It was no fluke. It was so very real. With the dance at the junior high where Joe attended, kids paid to be there, and the school donated the space. This was the first time we were around our kids' teachers and peers since the diagnosis, and I felt we were looked at differently. It wasn't inherently bad or too uncomfortable, but we were no longer Jay and Rachel Mitlo. We had become Jay and Rachel Mitlo, those poor parents who were dealing with a child with cancer. To be fair, that's exactly who we were. In that role at that event, we had the opportunity to be there and thank everyone. There were many to thank as many people were involved.

There always seemed to be a fundraiser going on. For us, it was certainly humbling. People we knew and many people we didn't know would be involved. It was a constant reminder that these were different times, but people did care and would not leave us feeling alone. It was great to see people we didn't expect to show us their love and support. It was always a bit embarrassing, but that was overshadowed by our appreciation of the love.

Early in the winter of 2014, we knew that, barring the miracle that we had been praying for coming true, Trey wouldn't be with us for too much longer. I didn't want Joe and Bella's next memory of Trey to be of his passing. I'll share more on what transpired in the months leading up to that winter and about the miracle that we had been praying for as well in later chapters. But it was the result of all of this that led to creating a fundraiser myself. I will talk more about our trips and vacations in chapter 12, but we wanted to go back to Disney. We had done a Make-A-Wish trip in 2012, but Trey was limited due to his age and condition at the time. It was our desire to create a beautiful memory with all three kids that led me to create a fundraiser. This was the only fundraiser I organized. I wrote out a crowdsourcing letter and began a campaign with the goal of raising $8,000 for our trip. We raised that amount the night we launched it. It was over $12,000 by the next afternoon. I say all of that to say this: Rachel was overwhelmed and, to a degree, embarrassed by the outpouring of love. At one point, she exclaimed, "Shut it down!!!" As I went to do just that, several more texts and emails came in. Each and every one of them stated things like, "Don't you dare turn this off! People want to give. They want to be a part of blessing you. Don't rob them of that opportunity." So, I prayed and listened to everyone and left it up for a few more days. Rachel understood that people wanted to be a part of something remarkable. Regardless of your politics, it's amazing and surreal when a guy like Donald Trump makes a contribution to your child and family, which he most certainly did.

We were always amazed at how people organized, contributed, and donated. It did make a huge difference in the day-to-day life that we had to endure. It was so nice to be able to give my children (all of them) gifts we had received or been provided with the means to purchase. Never worrying about having to pay our bills while we were worrying about the lives of our family was a huge relief. We are so very grateful to everyone who helped us.

## How To Stand

No matter who you are, fundraisers are essential to getting through a child being diagnosed with a life-threatening disease. Even millionaires need the support and community engagement that come with these events. There should be no shame in being the beneficiary. Each parent needs to be mindful as to how they are involved. Some parents will be more comfortable being at the center of the fundraisers, others much less. It is my opinion that fundraisers should happen no matter what. If neither parent wants to be involved, then someone very close should be taking the point in at least being aware of the fundraisers and giving them an opportunity to occur.

With that being said, if you are a parent who is involved in the fundraising, be careful about how much time and energy you spend on it. This involvement could give you a renewed sense of life and purpose and be a healthy distraction from the day-to-day grind. More often, though, I fear that the parent who wants to run these is running away from the tougher challenges that she or he must face. If you are seeking control in a life that has gone well beyond any semblance of order, this activity is not going to help. You should always have input and veto power, but to run these events takes too much time away from other areas where you are needed.

It is, however, important for at least one parent to show up as often as possible when the event takes place. Shy away from taking the whole family all the time. It can become a circus and create more unnecessary emotions. Whoever is best in front of people should take the lead and represent the entire family. If there is a sibling who needs additional attention, by all means, take that child. It's all about meeting each person's needs in the most trying time of their life.

I mentioned above that there was a fundraiser at a local brewery. Being in ministry, one might think we would have a problem or conflict with that. We did not. Again, if the people in their battle do have a problem with beer, raffles, bingo, golf, or whatever, then don't do it. There is enough stress and conflict going around without adding another through the events that are meant to support.

Lastly, it is my advice and experience to shy away from multi-tiered marketing campaigns where "x" percent goes to you. It just feels a bit transactional and cumbersome. If you are getting 100 percent of the proceeds, that's much better. If it doesn't bother you, though, feel free to move forward.

Fundraisers are most likely going to happen, and if they do, that's a good thing. Just do your best not to allow them to turn into a bad thing.

Perhaps no one is offering to do any fundraising for you. If you (or they) have decided to keep this much more private, you will find this to be the case. If that's the case, you're probably okay with the lack of attention. On the other hand, you might desire to stay somewhat private but need the money. This presents a challenging situation. If the need for money outweighs the desire for privacy, you will most likely need to move forward.

Given your desire for privacy, the further away from you that the organizer of the event is, the better off you'll be. There may be business groups like Rotary or social organizations like Shriner's that you could reach out to for help. Again, the social workers at the hospital may be a resource that could help you.

## How To Help Them Stand

Here is where those who are watching from a bit of a distance can really shine. All it takes is a quick phone call to whoever is on point for fundraising, and you can be a huge asset to the family by having a fundraiser for them. Once you've received the okay, organize it, staff it, run it, and bless the family! Maybe that's not within your skill set. If that's the case, attend every fundraiser that you can. Very often, these fundraisers need workers. These positions are initially filled with people the organizers know. However, often they need more bodies to make it a success. You can be one of the nameless, faceless angels that make these events run smoothly and raise much-needed funds.

## To overzealous pastors and any others who like to be in control:

I heard of a pastor who called a church member into the office to review a fundraising campaign this member's family was having for their loved one. The pastor grilled the poor guy as to why he was not consulted and why this guy felt that he could just reach out to the congregation without the pastor's permission. The pastor was aggressive, angry, and entirely negligent to the person he was called to shepherd.

It's not always pastors. There are those who "have been through this" and want to do it their way. There are those who have opinions on the morality or styles of certain fundraisers. They like to exert their stance and make it known as to what is and isn't acceptable.

Don't be these people. You may think you're helping. You are not. You might think you're protecting them. You are not. At the very least, you are imposing your own need for respect or attention on these people in their time of need and suffering. You are probably elevating your values above their needs. Worst of all, you are further complicating the most complicated time of their lives. You are also doing the opposite of your intention; you are hurting instead of helping.

To my brothers and sisters in Christ who, again, want to defend the purity of the faith and keep this family from sinning by holding a "questionable" fundraiser: it's just not your place. That sounds harsh, but it's really not. These are people in the fight of and for their lives (literally their child's life). Even if the event is clearly beyond what you believe to be permissible given their proclaimed faith, it will not help for you to object. IF . . . if they ask for your opinion or guidance, feel free to *gently* give it. Otherwise, stay out of it. They have way too much going on at this time.

# CHAPTER 10

# It's Okay to Laugh

I WAS WALKING OUT OF A STORE IN A SHOPPING CENTER WHEN A MAN APPROACHED ME. He had a ticket package for the Pirates, and for only this many dollars, I could get to go to this many games. I was in no way going to give this guy any of my information, nor was I going to buy tickets in a parking lot. However, I'm not confrontational (as much as I'd like to be in my "tough guy" mind) and didn't want this interaction to be drawn out further with his retorts to my reluctance. Then, it hit me. How can I buy tickets when my child has cancer? I was living day to day, hour to hour. That was my out! I simply said to him, "This really sounds like a good deal, but my son was just diagnosed with cancer. I have no idea what my life looks like moving forward, and I certainly can't commit to buying baseball tickets." You would have thought I told him that I had a deadly infectious disease. His face went pale, he began to stutter, and he backed away from me while apologizing profusely. I actually chuckled as he left . . . in a hurry.

I had discovered something powerful at that moment. I would later call it the C-Card. If I was ever in a tight spot, a terrible conversation, or an awkward social situation where something ridiculous was being asked of me, I would simply play the C-Card. It would vary and depend on the circumstance. In one instance where I was being asked to do something I didn't want to do, I would just say that I couldn't due to Trey's cancer. Other times, if I was in an unbearable conversation with a stranger, I would gently slip in the fact that my son had cancer. Not once did they want to continue the conversation. While this is certainly a negative experience, having (almost) everyone not know what to say or do around you could just occasionally be a positive thing.

Rachel and I were at a friend's party where I was explaining the C-Card to some people. At the party was one of the oncologists who knew Trey and us. He wasn't one of Trey's main doctors, but we certainly knew and liked him. After I finished explaining the C-Card, I said, "Look, there are very few perks to having a child with cancer. I'm going to use every one of them that I can." With his drink to his lips, the doctor (not really a part of the conversation but well within earshot) slowly looked at me and nodded in approval. It was such a great and underrated moment for us. He knew and understood us, and he confirmed not only what we were saying but also how we were approaching things. To be fair and clear, Rachel never used the C-Card intentionally. It just wasn't for her. Understand this as well: she very often benefited from me using it, oftentimes *for* her. It just wasn't something she was going to use. Remember, each person in this horrific time is different and has different needs and ways of coping.

One afternoon, I had left the hospital with a little time before I had to pick Joe and Bella up from school. We had been given some money to bless the kids, so I went to buy the older two each a Nintendo DS. The clerk asked me, "How many kids do you have?" It made sense since I was buying two of the same units.

When I replied, "Three," she asked, "If two of them are getting a DS, what is the third one getting?"

I answered (without thinking at all) "Cancer. He's got cancer."

You would have thought I had snapped my pinky off to pay for the games. She was white as a ghost and began to apologize profusely. Realizing what I had just put her through, I began to do the same. She couldn't get me out of there fast enough. The entire exchange was so ridiculous that I simply had to laugh . . . hard. I did feel terrible about what I had done to her but also knew I was just trying to get by.

You see, we had to laugh. We were certainly crying as well. It seems that the crying grew more infrequent as time went by, but when we did, it was harder and harder. If we didn't laugh sometimes, I'm quite sure that a deeper darkness would have set in.

Given that Trey had his "crayons," and they couldn't ever be messed with, his sleeping became a battle. While he was in bed,

Trey would unzip his pajamas and take off the protective netting. That would leave those "crayons" unprotected and vulnerable to breaking, and that would ensure a quick emergency trip to the hospital. This was a classic Trey "stinker" moment. We ended up using extra-strong duct tape to adhere the zipper to the pajamas, and then more of the same along the zipper track in case he was able to pull the zipper free. We would be lying in bed and we'd hear the clicking and clacking back and forth of his "crayons" on his crib-bed railing. Time and time again, he would free himself from his adhesive pajama prison and run the "crayons" across the rails like a prisoner with a tin cup in his jail cell. Exactly what do you do with that? You laugh. Here was the poor child, riddled with cancer, defying both medical advice and common sense as well as his parents' directions and preventions . . . to simply stand naked and declare his freedom.

With chemotherapy comes nausea. Sometimes there was less, sometimes a lot more. Trey would be sitting in his high chair eating his meal and we would hear the gurgle. Trey would yell, "I need my bucket!!!" Sometimes we got it to him in time, but sometimes we didn't. It is said that the fastest way to wake up in the morning is to hear your dog or cat beginning to vomit. I would argue that hearing "I need my bucket" elicits a greater response. Very often, his exclamation would be joined by either Joe or Bella screaming, "He's going to puke!" Rachel and I would come flying from whatever part of the house we were in, crashing into whatever was in our way. If we didn't make it, the tray of his highchair would be the landing place. However, also due to his being on steroids, more often than not, his appetite was incredible. So, we would simply clear the tray, clean it, add more food, and start all over. Every so often, the ridiculousness of the situation and stage of life we were in would hit us, and we would just stop and laugh. We still laugh about it to this day.

Trey, as mentioned above, didn't love clothes. You could blame it on his "crayons," but even after they were removed, he very often liked to go commando. Perhaps that's true of all two-to-six-year-olds. He was still just a kid, after all. We once had all the family over at our house for a party of some sort. It is important to remember that life and normalcy have to go on. We heard a loud commotion downstairs where the kids were playing. One by one, with the oldest coming first, the kids ran from the top of the steps, through the kitchen and dining room, and upstairs, terrified and screaming. Who was the last one up the stairs? Yes, it was the poor, bald, sick child riddled with cancer. Why were they, and he, running? Well, you see, it was because he was completely naked (his "crayons" and protective netting intact) and chasing them. How does one not laugh at that? It was, at least for the adults, a great reminder that it's not all doom and gloom. You have to laugh, or at least you should.

It wasn't always times at home or with family that made us laugh. Sometimes others were blessed to join us. Trey had the need for continuing tests and outpatient treatments on a very regular basis. We would go to the ninth-floor clinic at CHP, where Trey loved to entertain the nurses. There was a young nurse named Mindy who Trey named "Mindy Lou Who." Trey was very fond of her. Every time we were there, Trey had to get a blood draw. When the tube was filled, Trey would shake it up and call it his "blood shake." That may be odd, but it's not the funny part. One time, Mindy Lou Who was bent over by his feet doing something. Trey reached out and slid the "blood shake" tube directly . . . into her cleavage, saying, "There you go, Mindy Lou Who." I would like for you to imagine how you would respond to your terminally ill child doing something so very inappropriate. For the record, Mindy Lou Who joined us in nervous laughter. Like just about everyone else who interacted with Trey, she not only cared for his needs as a patient but loved Trey for being Trey.

## How To Stand

What can you do? You are in for a long and drawn-out battle. There will be many moments where you want to laugh. You may have the feeling that this is no time for laughter. You may feel guilty for laughing. Grace has got to be given to those in this battle. I very well may have ruined that clerk's day when I was buying the games for Joe and Bella. I certainly didn't intend to, but it was very likely traumatic for her. I could have chosen to weep in the parking lot due to the situation that I was in and that I had just put her in. Other times I may very well have. This time, though, I just laughed.

Laughter, in many ways, is the counterbalance to crying. If all we do is cry, we end up in a very dark place. Trust me; there is more than enough darkness to go around. It's okay to laugh. Yes, you can't laugh at everything and use it as an avoidance of the severity of the situation. Trust me; everyone is most likely aware of the situation you are in. Even if they are not, whatever you are feeling is okay.

If you're having trouble finding anything to laugh about during these times, it's more than understandable. Try to take even just a few minutes to entertain yourself with your favorite funny (for heaven's sake, not sad) movies or television shows. Go to what has made you laugh in the past and see if you can lighten the mood even just for a bit. Hopefully, in your plan for Standing in these times, you've included a strategic friend or two who maybe isn't the best at comfort but is always good for a laugh.

If you find that you haven't laughed at all, and can't, it's okay. It's okay . . . at least to a point. These are obviously the worst times you have ever experienced. However, if you are only experiencing the pain and sadness and you haven't noticed any joy, let alone laughter, it may be time to get some help. The enemy is trying to destroy your family in many ways. Getting professional help is one way to combat that. Good therapy can be essential to getting through these times and in no way, shape, or form is a sign of weakness. Hopefully, you have someone around you (as mentioned in chapter 2) who is making sure you are okay. If they have noticed that you are not doing well, they're probably right. Remember, if you're not okay (or the parents aren't), then the family isn't going to be okay, either.

## How To Help Them Stand

If you are coming alongside the person in their battle, feel whatever they are feeling. These are mostly helpless times. If you can help them to not feel alone and appreciate the moment for what it is, you have helped them in a great way. If they are laughing, laugh with them. If they think that something is ridiculous and are shaking their head, shake yours too. When they are around you, allow them to be the people they genuinely are; they shouldn't have to pretend when they are with you.

It's okay to share funny memes or videos with them as well. Certainly think and pray about it first and watch their reactions. If they appreciate it, send them more. If they let you know that it wasn't funny to them, back off for a bit. Laughing is very much okay, but not to be forced. Keeping them from feeling alone is the key.

Furthermore, if the parents or loved ones around the child in their battle are the only ones laughing, they can be left feeling very alone and judged. You do not need to remind them of the severity of the situation. They do not need to be scolded for having a nervous release of energy at an inappropriate moment. You are strategically placed in their lives to help them, come alongside them, and join them as best you can. Guiding, directing, and correcting their outlook is not any of those things.

# CHAPTER 11

# The Ugly Part(s)

WHEN YOU HAVE A CHILD DIAGNOSED WITH A LIFE-THREATENING CONDITION, IT'S (UNDERSTATEMENT) UGLY. Yes, there are many bright spots and moments of blessings. However, one cannot overlook the fact that there are many times that you have to go through the worst to see the best.

When we first went up to the ninth (cancer) floor, I remember looking at the kids in cages. No, they weren't actual cages. They were beds that had railings that went to the ceiling, effectively making them cages. Yes, the railings could and did come down, but they looked like cages. I remember thinking, *Man, I feel bad for the kids who have to be in those.* Yep, our kid would be one of those. Every kid under "x" years old is a fall risk and thus has to have the bars up when they sleep or are unattended. It's terrible. Even worse, many of the bars would stick or squeak, so just when Trey would fall asleep, we would wake him by putting up the rails. Good times.

Shortly after (or before?) his first chemo treatment, we had his hair cut off. I say "after or before" because I don't remember. There were a lot of details and specifics that just escape my mind. As it was, we didn't want it to slowly clump out and look so horrific. We wanted to avoid Joe and Bella seeing that and, frankly, we wanted to get it over with. Our good friend Kelly owns Kindred Curls salon and came by to shave Trey's head. In our living room, Trey was becoming one of those bald kids who I had prayed for when we first started coming to the hospital. The chemo would also ultimately take his eyebrows and any hair anywhere else on his body. When he went through the most aggressive treatments, his eyes would sink and his skin would grow pale. It was horrifying how many different looks he had over those four years.

When we first came home after his first round of chemo, it was my job to give him his daily shot. You read that right: I HAD TO GIVE MY SON A DAILY SHOT! When you leave the hospital with your newborn child, you think, *You're just trusting me with them?* Let me tell you . . . being entrusted with administering medicine to your child through a hypodermic needle is a whole other level. Rachel swaddled him up in a blanket so that his legs and arms were bound. We exposed the skin, and I went for it. Rachel screamed.

"I CAN'T BELIEVE THAT YOU SCREAMED!" I yelled at Rachel.

"I CAN'T BELIEVE YOU STUCK HIM WITH THAT!" Rachel replied.

We both laughed (see previous chapter), and we both cried. Oh, yeah . . . Trey didn't like it, either. During chemo, this was a regular and daily part of our lives—the shots, not the screaming. Trey got used to it. That's ugly too. No kid should get used to that. No parent should, either.

Trey's Broviac line (yep, the source of the "crayons") came out of his chest and was a direct line to his bloodstream. Since possible infection was the greatest threat besides the cancer, the "crayons" were sealed under a clear bandage with only the lines coming out. Once a week, the sealed bandage area had to be changed, and that was Rachel's responsibility. It took great care and attention to detail to accomplish, and those were her strengths. The nurses always marveled at her work and said she was the best parent they'd seen in keeping that area clean. In order to keep it sterile, the adhesive they used was extremely (even more than you would imagine) strong. Beyond that, it turned out that Trey was allergic to the adhesive, and his skin would turn bright red where the bandage was attached to his chest. It was sheer agony to him when we had to take it off. He would go heels to head, arching his back from the pain. As with the shots, we would have to swaddle him up so that he couldn't flail about. Mind you, if he broke one of his "crayons" or somehow broke the skin in this fiasco, we would have to be rushed to the hospital. Of all the things he went through, this was among the worst in regard to pain . . . and WE had to do it to him.

Early on, after one or two rounds of chemo, Trey had a surgical procedure with the goal of removing as many of the tumors as possible. They knew they couldn't get them all but wanted to give the chemo fewer tumors to fight. Unfortunately, they had to stop the surgery sooner than they wanted to because his kidney was shutting down, and the medical team feared that they might lose it. More on that later.

Very often, Trey had to get images taken to see how much cancer was present and where it was located. It was a lot like an MRI with the giant tube. To keep him motionless but not unconscious, they would give him Versed (a lot like Valium). We called it "silly juice." Within seconds of him taking it, he was like the most pleasant drunk you'd ever been around. Very often, it worked the first time, but many times it did not. He would still be wiggling, laughing, crying, whatever. We could be in that imaging center for thirty minutes . . . or three hours. He got frustrated, we got frustrated . . . it was ugly.

One time, he had to drink this horrific liquid before some test. It was thick and smelly, and clearly it did not taste good. I had taken Joe and Bella to school, and then I met Trey and Rachel in the prep room. They were both done with it. No, they weren't done with the procedure or the liquid. They were done with each other, the process, the morning, the everything. I came to the rescue. I would get him to drink it all. I sprang into action, and he downed two-thirds of it in no time. Then, he remembered and reminded me that he was done. Rachel was in the corner reading. Trey was crying. I was holding him and saying over and over again, "I know, buddy; I know." He finally grabbed my face with both hands, looked into my eyes, and said, "NO, YOU DON'T!"

Holy crap, I did not. Who was I to say that I knew what he was going through? I didn't even know what it tasted like, let alone what it was like to be him in this time. I don't remember what I said, but he finished the drink and got the image taken. What I do remember is that the whole ordeal was ugly.

We were told that a certain type of chemo he was going to receive would turn his urine red and that we should not be alarmed. It could even turn his tears red. Sure enough, his pee became red, and we did our best not to be alarmed. However, his tears did not become red. I was kind of bummed about that. Why would I want my son's tears to be red? To be brutally honest, I'm not really sure. I guess it would have been one side effect that wouldn't hurt him and was, for lack of a better term, crazy. Who has red tears? We were told to wear gloves when we changed his diaper as the residual chemo in his urine would burn our hands. Clearly, I never wore gloves—I'm a man's man, after all, and lazy. Sure enough, if I got even a trace of it on my hands, it would tingle or burn. How did it not cause him pain rubbing against his skin? Later on I would consider that to be one of the many miracles we *did* get. I was even excited for the nasty raccoons that were always tearing through our garbage to get a mouth full of a chemo diaper. Sadly, they did . . . and it didn't faze them. At least they didn't turn into radioactive zombie raccoons. I digress; back to the ugly.

Several times Trey had to get a sample of his spinal fluid taken from him. Basically, they would take a medical corkscrew and dig into his spine. They told us that many parents throw up if they watch or even stay in the room for the procedure. Seeing the corkscrew alone gave me the heebie jeebies. Rachel could not and would not be there for those, so I would stay with Trey in the room while they did what they had to do. I don't remember if I watched or not at the beginning; I feel like I did the second time. It was bad, but I made it. The thing is, these procedures didn't bother Trey at all. Sometimes things were worse for us, at least emotionally, than they were for him.

Trey had one surgery early on and one later that year. Both times, we had to spend a lot of time in the waiting room. On the one hand, these were the ugliest of times, but not for why we would think. It was ugly because of everyone else that was there. At 7:00 a.m. there's a five-year-old drinking a bottle of Mountain Dew and eating chips. A mother and her three kids are fighting with each other and running all over the place. The TV is on, playing the worst morning talk show in the history of broadcasting. Everyone smells. You look for the number indicating Trey going from "triage" to "prep" to "in surgery" to "recover" and it just doesn't move. Oh, yeah, and your kid has cancer and might die. Ugly.

The second surgery brought the ugliest moments for us. The chemo was not working. They were going in to remove as many of the tumors as they could, telling us that it would take twenty to forty-four hours to complete. I remember being there the morning of the surgery and realizing that this was a big deal. Everyone took notice of us. Surgeons, anesthesiologists, nurses, and doctors came up to us to introduce themselves and say it was an "honor" to work on our son. I realized then that this surgery was an anomaly, and things weren't necessarily what we thought they were. I figured out that this was a Hail Mary operation . . . on my son. It seemed that this wasn't something they had successfully accomplished before, and I remember wondering if each of them was thinking, *If this works, I'm going to be written about and be famous.* I asked the surgeon what the worst-case scenario was in regard to the results of the surgery.

"We don't get all of the cancer," he replied.

I asked, "But nothing else? Nothing catastrophic?"

He said, "Well, there's always the chance of bleeding out, but there's no reason to believe that will happen; it's very rare."

The surgery began, and Rachel and I did the typical dance of avoiding as many annoying people in the waiting room as possible. At lunch, we went for a walk to a nearby pizza place. We got a phone call from a nurse telling us that Trey had lost one of his kidneys (we knew that this was most likely going to happen). We thought something worse had happened. It did occur to me that the news of our child losing a kidney was no big deal to us. How ugly is that? Once we were off the phone, we actually made fun of how long it took the nurse to tell us that news that would normally have been considered devastating.

Later that day, everything changed. The surgeon came in, and he looked like five miles of bad road. I figured that they did not get all the tumors, as it had only been twelve or so hours out of the twenty-hour minimum they had advised. His first words were, "It did not go well. We almost lost Trey." I actually thought they had misplaced him. As it turns out, during the surgery they nicked his aorta. This was expected and in and of itself not a big deal. However, when the surgeon went to stitch it up, the aorta was like papier-mâché. Whether it was from the cancer or the chemo, the walls of Trey's aorta were so thin that the stitches went right through it. The surgeon called in a cardiac specialist, and they put a GORE-TEX patch over Trey's damaged aorta and sewed him back up. Trey was in intensive care. He might not be able to walk again. His remaining kidney might not function. He was in a medically induced coma. He was put through hell . . . and we signed him up for it.

Rachel asked me in one of our most horrific moments together, "What does this mean?"

I replied, "The day that we feared might one day come looks like it's going to come . . . but it wasn't today." We still had our son and were about to go in and see him.

They said that Trey "looked good," but I knew better. We walked in, and he was a mess, just as I'd thought. We spent some time with him, and then I began to make phone calls and texts giving people updates and asking for prayers. The next day, or maybe two days later, we took Joe and Bella in to see him. We told them as much as they could handle and prepared them the best we could. As Bella walked in and looked at Trey, she said, "Wow, he's all banged up." Yeah, when you get married and dream of life with a family, this is not what you expect. Gosh, it was so ugly. A day or two later, as Rachel was singing to Trey, a tear rolled down his face. He was coming out of it. He was responding to his mother's voice and touch. I described that moment as "beautifully horrific." Many things were that way in those days.

After the kids and Rachel left, I had a moment with "Sheriff Pete" and asked him how much time we had left with Trey now that the hope of the cancer being removed was gone. He hemmed and hawed, and he then said that cancer does what cancer wants to do . . . and that there was no timeline. I did not accept that answer. I had always been very kind, calm, and relational with him, but for this one moment, I stopped being that way.

"HOW MUCH TIME DO WE HAVE?" I asked quite aggressively, especially for me.

"One year, maybe two," he finally relented.

Okay then. I knew I couldn't tell Rachel or just about anyone else about this conversation. I was just going to have to deal with that one myself. Ugly.

It was at this point that we decided we would wait no longer to live and enjoy Trey's life. We didn't know how much time we had left with him and weren't going to wait around for him to be 100 percent, as that probably wasn't going to happen. We decided that next summer was going to be "The Summer of Trey." We would take our Make-A-Wish trip, we would travel, and we would go to any amusement park possible. However, that would have to wait.

As he did time and time again, Trey rallied. His remaining kidney kicked into full gear, he wasn't the least bit paralyzed, and he was discharged within a week. At his checkup a month later, the doctor asked us, "Has Trey been different? Has he been lethargic? Has he turned blue at all?" I certainly would have put "turning blue" into acting differently. It turned out that one of his lungs had collapsed. Trey being the "Young Warrior" had shown no signs of that at all. So, we were again admitted, and they put in a half-inch chest tube to drain the fluid that was in his pleural space; that is the area between the lungs and chest wall. We learned a lot during those days. When the time came for the tube to come out, they brought in two doctors to remove it. Not a doctor and a nurse or aid . . . but two doctors. They let me know that this was going to be painful for Trey. The second doctor said, "Oh, he's going to cry . . . a lot." (Thanks, Doc.) While one doctor held Trey down, the other pulled the tube. Trey said in an eerily confident and quiet voice, "No." It was a simple, defiant statement. No tears. No crying. Nothing else. I believe he was saying both, "No, I don't like this" and "No, I will not cry for you today." This was another unsung miracle moment.

After that new kind of traumatic moment, we were released, but he had to be put on a zero (not low) fat diet. His lung had collapsed due to chyle (fat droplets) leaking from somewhere. Thus, they wanted to make sure his lung didn't collapse again until they could monitor it and figure out why it had happened. This was the worst part of his entire cancer treatment as far as we were concerned. He was fine. He was normal. He was recovering from a life-threatening surgery that had gone bad. Now I couldn't feed him normal food? Now I had to tell him he couldn't have butter on his toast? He was crying, begging us for real food. He was wasting away. We finally went in for his checkup and the triage nurse (a wonderful if not a bit surly older lady) looked at us over her glasses after weighing him and said, "You know he only twenty-eight pounds?"

"Yes, ma'am, we are more than aware of it." As it turns out, they had punctured something in the failed surgery, and that was the cause of the chyle leak. He was back up and running and gaining weight in no time.

From there, things got a lot better. Sure, there were setbacks and complications. Eventually, we even had him go to a radiation treatment where he was put in a concrete-fortified room and blasted with so much radiation that everything he took into the room with him would have to be destroyed afterward. Rachel was only allowed to go into the room for a few minutes a day, and even then she had to wear a coat of lead armor to protect her. Trey handled it all with great courage and strength. It seems that the surgery and subsequent complications were a bit of a turning point. There would still be ugly moments, but we would see many more blessings through those challenging times.

## How To Stand

When someone is told that their child may die, it's the scariest news they may ever hear (other than them actually dying). To have to come face to face with your greatest fears is an obviously ugly truth of this situation. However, it is far from the only ugliness one will face.

- The day-to-day complications are maddening.

- The pain of the treatment can be just as bad as the disease, and sometimes worse.

- The changes to the body of your child can be visible and traumatizing.

- The day-to-day grind of treatments, procedures, and maintenance can be a slow drip of torture for the child . . . and for you.

- Watching your child suffer while knowing that they may not make it is horrific.

- Having to care for your child and at the same time inflicting literal physical pain makes no sense.

- Relationships can be very strained during these times (praise God we were spared this), and many marriages don't make it.

- Watching others suffer (siblings of the sick child, grandparents, friends, etc.) is really difficult for the parents as well.

- Realizing that no one cares for your child (hospital staff, teachers, or even other family) as much as you do is sobering.

- Seeing your child overcome so much is heartwarming, beautiful, and inspiring. It's also heartbreaking.

- Very often, there will be curveballs and unforeseen tragedies that come out of nowhere. The diagnosis only being the beginning is daunting and frightening.

# How To Help Them Stand

Be the one who accepts the parents' emotions as valid . . . no matter what. Allow them to be however they are. Don't tell them not to feel that way. Saying something like, "Don't cry!" is not helpful. Likewise, don't point out the "good" in any situation or how God is working. "God has a plan!" He does have a plan, but right now they need comfort and not perspective. When you join them in their emotions, you can help them Stand. At the same time, don't stop talking with them at all.

Please don't tell them how you've faced similar pain in your life. You may be trying to show them that you understand, but instead you are taking the focus away from them. We call this "stealing their story." Instead, try to feel what they are feeling. Join them in whatever pain they are in. It won't cure or fix the situation, but it will help keep them from feeling alone. Helping them to feel a sense of connection is one of the keys to helping them Stand.

Stay as close to them as they allow you to be. Do not swarm them, but always be open to hearing their stories. If they want or are willing to be distracted, enable them. Give them time away from the grind. Do what you can to make their life as normal as possible.

Give them as much control as they want. Always give them options and choices rather than directives or blank, open offers. Look at these examples:

- "I can pick up the groceries for the week if you'd like or go with you to the store."

- "Would you like me to take the kids Friday, Saturday, or not at all?"

- Don't say, "Let me know if you need anything." Be more specific.

- "The fundraiser raised $2K; let me know when you want it, or I can just hold on to it."

As often as possible (if you're so inclined), pray for wisdom on how to keep them from feeling alone. Above all else, be there with them. Don't observe them, don't counsel them, and don't try to fix them. Just do your best to be present with them.

## Christians ... take note:

It bears repeating that you do not need to be God's public relations director. You may feel like you have to defend God at every turn of this family's tragedy. You'll "feel led" to give them a proper perspective on what is happening. You'll want to give them Scripture that will adjust how they are thinking and change their focus. You might want to remind them to have faith, to pray, or to read their Bible so that they don't (continue to) stray. You will have the best of intentions, but it will not do what you want it to do. Instead, it will either cause them to resent and distance themselves from you or leave them feeling guilty and like a bad Christian. Read through Job in the Bible and see the mistakes that those closest to him made. Then see how God reacted to them.

What they need is someone to be there with them. They need to not be alone during this time. Romans 12:15 says to "mourn with those who mourn." It does not say, "Flood them with Scripture verses and religious platitudes." Yet, that's what many Christians do during these times. Resist that urge. God is more than aware of the situation they are in. He has strategically placed you in their life to love and serve them, to pray for them, to suffer alongside them, but not to correct or redirect them.

CHAPTER 12

# Trips Are Not Vacations

W E CALLED IT "THE SUMMER OF TREY" AFTER HIS
FAILED SURGERY AND NEAR-DEATH EXPERIENCE IN
THE FALL OF 2011—HIS FIRST YEAR IN TREATMENT. As I type
this, I feel uneasy, as I never wanted anything to appear as if it
was centered only around Trey. The intent was never to leave
Joe and Bella feeling overlooked. I suppose we didn't call it
"The Summer of Trey" around them, only on social media.
Regardless, the pressure to protect Joe and Bella at all costs
was (and is) always there.

As soon as Trey was stabilized, we contacted Make-A-
Wish, the nonprofit that arranges to grant wishes (for us, a
trip) for kids with critical illnesses. We were assigned a trip
ambassador who we actually knew! Diane had her own battle
with a child with cancer and knew our story very well. We had
the orientation meeting and planned our trip to Disney! We
stayed at a place called Give Kids the World Village. It is an

amazing place and yet another organization that exists solely to create great experiences for families facing life-threatening diagnoses. It was started by a hotelier who would donate rooms to Make-A-Wish families. As the story goes, one time he didn't have enough rooms, and neither did any other hotels, and a family lost their child before they could get their wish. Wanting to make sure that this never happened again, he organized, fundraised, collaborated, designed, and built Give Kids the World Village. We headed to Orlando during the last week of February 2012.

The village consists of many unique and storybook-style cottages in a neighborhood setting. There are pools, water parks, playgrounds, and a fishing hole. All of this is centered around a main street where there are shops, a main dining area, a carousel, a theater, and the very famous ice cream shop where kids can get ice cream whenever they want. One of their mottos is actually "Ice Cream for Breakfast!" Each child (siblings included) gets a wrapped gift every day they are there. There are many activities and shows throughout the week to entertain all ages. It is said that some kids have wanted to stay in the Village rather than go to the amusement parks that Give Kids the World has agreements with in the Orlando area (Disney, Universal Studios, Sea World, Legoland, etc.). We planned out two trips to Disney, one to Sea World, and one to Legoland. It was going to be great. It was going to be memorable. It was going to be a lot—an awful lot of doing.

When we first arrived at the Village, we were blown away. So much thought and detail went into making the experience both as simple and as memorable as possible. Our cottage was right next to the playground, as Trey loved to play. Since he couldn't swim (his "crayons" couldn't get wet), we didn't want to be by a pool. As it was, the playground was being repaired and was closed. We were in the process of getting accustomed to setbacks; we didn't let it bother us and headed to dinner. What we experienced next was a moment, one of many, that was far more for us than it was for the kids.

We sat down in the very busy (both in number of people and how it was decorated) dining room. Every little thing was carefully thought out. The dining room, like everything in the Village, was so creative, interactive, entertaining, and simply fun. I looked around the room at all of the families and realized that for the first time in almost eighteen months, we weren't special. We did not stand out. *Everyone* there was "like us." We were all in the middle of the battle of a lifetime. I had never sensed such a feeling of community as I did in that moment. Then, I looked around again at the decorations and noticed something else . . . the volunteers. So many people were there by their own charity, not being paid a single penny. My aunt and uncle who lived in Florida were there as well. The room that was incredibly loud with the sounds of laughter, talking, and the occasional scream or cry (you can't have everything) had gotten surreally quiet. At least, the noise had faded away for me. I just stared around the room at the volunteers, the other families, MY family, and the decorations. So much intentionality was focused on giving us the gift of memories. I teared up hard and choked back the emotions to save my family from wondering what was wrong with Dad (this was a common battle I had to face).

The next day, we had breakfast where some of the Disney characters would be, and, of course, Trey flipped out and didn't want to be around them. Again, not everything goes as well as it should, but that's okay. We adjusted and moved forward. We got on the monorail and headed to the Magic Kingdom. We were all excited, but apparently Trey was more excited than all of us. As we rounded the last bend and the park was visible, Trey screamed, "There it is! There it is! There's Cinderella's castle!!!" It was so loud that the entire tram became silent. After what seemed like a minute but was probably only three seconds, Trey said in a very calm but inquisitive voice, "Too loud?" Everyone erupted in laughter.

We took all the pictures and experienced all the weather (hot, rain, chilly, humid). We ate all the food and ran as fast as we could. You cannot call it a vacation in any sense, but it was a trip that began many of what I would call "mental snapshots." We might not have Trey forever, but we would have these memories.

One of the many perks from Give Kids the World is that you receive an amusement park "passport." For one calendar year, you get free admission to any of the many participating amusement parks in the country. It seemed "The Summer of Trey" was only beginning.

Later that spring, Trey got the first good medical news he'd had in a long time. He was getting his "crayons" removed! Given that he was no longer going to be getting chemo (it hadn't worked as we'd hoped), they were no longer needed. Besides the annoyances and agony of changing them, the worst part of

Trey's "crayons" was that he could not go swimming with those IV lines still in play. With them being surgically removed, he was free to swim! You might think, *How is another surgery part of the good medical news?* Other than revisiting the trauma of six months earlier (which was very real), this step was no big deal.

We immediately planned a trip to Great Wolf Lodge, a hotel and water park made for families. This was a trip that was perfect for Trey, Joe, Bella, and me. Oh, Rachel? No, this would not be her cup of tea at all. However, it would also not be the first or last time one of us sacrificed our personal desires or comforts for the good of the family. Rachel did a great job of pretending she was happy to be there (which to a degree she was). The kids had the time of their lives!

Trey kept mostly to the "little kid" area, sliding down and climbing up the mini slides over and over again. Joe and I went down every slide they had while Bella and Rachel kept to the ones in the middle (not so scary but more than the kiddie slides). Then, Trey made his move. He came to the main center attraction, where Joe, Bella, and I were spending quite a bit of time. There were slides, climbing ropes, water guns, and a huge bucket that would dump water down every so often. Joe and Bella had gone down the slides of that tower countless times, and Trey was now ready to do the same. I stood there with him, encouraging him to make sure he kept straight and lay flat on his back. Shortly after he pushed off, he sat straight up and looked back at me. There was fear in his eyes, and in mine as well, I'm quite sure. There he was, sliding down in great peril, and I couldn't do anything to help him. Even here at a water park I was reminded of every other part of his life that I had no control over. I could hear his screams and even the sound of his body (and head) banging off of the sides of the slides as he went down. Rachel, waiting for him at the bottom, scooped him up and began to comfort him. Before we left, we made sure to have him go down the kiddie slides again. Again, we laughed, we played, we ate, we adventured, we spent a lot of money, and we had a great trip. It was not a vacation but a time of creating many mental snapshots.

With our Give Kids the World passport and the donation of a timeshare in Virginia, we headed to Busch Gardens, Water Country USA, and Virginia Beach. In a lot of ways, this was peak "Summer of Trey." We did it all. We went to an amusement park, a water park, the beach (we wanted Trey to see the ocean before . . .), and playgrounds.

Going to Virginia Beach was an odd moment. We wanted Trey to see the ocean, and he loved it. However, since we were just there for the day, we had to go to the main beach and park in the public parking. There were way too many people there, the beach was dirty, and we did not feel particularly safe. Joe, Bella, and Trey did not notice any of this one bit. It was another reminder that this was not, inherently, a time for Rachel and me other than getting to experience life and create memories. I remember a Band-Aid floating in the water next to the kids. For Rachel and me, Give Kids the World and the entire trip to Orlando was, dare I say it, magical. Now, our kids were swimming in dirty water near a littered beach and changing in a scary public bathroom. The kids? How did they feel about it? They had a great time. Memories.

Busch Gardens is an incredible amusement park. It's a mix of Cedar Point and Epcot Center, and far too big to tackle in one day. We actually went in the morning, headed back to the condo for nap time, and returned for the evening. In a way, it was this decision that showed that we had figured out how to do all of this. We both pushed the limits of exhaustion and knew when to draw back. We were getting the most out of each experience before ruining it out of fear of missing out. On a side note, it was here that Joe really rode some of his scariest "big boy" roller coasters for the first time. Each of the kids was growing up and hitting milestones, and we were purposeful not to miss any of them.

Water Country USA (the water park) was incredible in that it was everything the kids could have imagined. At the same time, it was a time of nervous anxiety for Rachel. We already had one child whose life was on the line. Why were we putting the other two in danger? This trip reminded us that's where life is. We couldn't put any of them in a bubble forever.

We surrounded the parks with dinners out (always an adventure), swimming in the condo's pool, and playing at local playgrounds. Joe got a terrible scratch on his back at one of these—just another reminder that we couldn't put the kids in a safety bubble. Oddly, one of my favorite memories of that trip is Trey sitting in the giant bathtub at the condo, talking on a phone (that was disconnected). He was happy, laughing, and silly. It was simple . . . just a kid having fun.

We certainly weren't on a vacation, but we were living life and creating memories.

There were always trips to Kennywood. Kennywood is the biggest amusement park in our town and one of the most historic in the United States. Trey absolutely loved going there. All of our kids loved it, and so did we as parents. We had season passes and would go for as long as we liked. It was incredible to see Trey not be able to ride something due to height restrictions and then months later be tall enough. As always, he never had fear. It was also great to see Rachel and Bella go their separate ways and go on rides that Bella loved. You never even knew if the kids would notice the individual time we took with each of them, making sure they knew that we cared for them and that they mattered. They may not have noticed, but it was important for us to make sure they didn't notice us not doing that.

Possibly one of the greatest moments of any trip came on our second trip to Great Wolf Lodge. This time we went to the one in the Poconos in northwest Pennsylvania (the first one was in Sandusky, Ohio). This lodge was larger and had more adventurous slides (more like Water Country), and that was perfect for Joe and Bella. However, the significant moment was with Trey, and it came early on. As we entered the water park, and without saying a word to us, Trey immediately and purposefully went over to the little kid slides. He went up and down a few times and then strode directly up to the exact same center slide where he had failed miserably the year before. It was the same setup in the Poconos and Sandusky. With arms crossed, body straight, and flat on his back, he perfectly slid down. He overcame his greatest fear and obstacle (as far as he knew . . . we knew he had overcome so many more at that point). From then on, the gloves were off and the restrictions were gone. He rode every ride there. It was almost like he had feared what had happened to him, and that fear was so foreign to him that he had to get rid of it. The biggest ride there had a very long line. At one point, Trey took matters into his own hands and loudly exclaimed, "The ride's broken! Everyone go back down!" It didn't work, but we all laughed. We also ate at an amazing New York-style pizza place (unless you're millionaires, you don't eat every meal at Great Wolf Lodge). There's nothing significant about that story except that it was really great food and a fun time for all of us. To a degree, that's all you ever really want, though.

Then there was the second Disney trip. I mentioned it in chapter 8, and it became the penultimate moment of our journey with Trey. EVERYONE was a part of us going. We had more than enough money to have the trip of a lifetime. We surprised the kids after school the day we left. We wanted it to blow their minds. As they screamed with joy and hugged Rachel, Trey stopped and asked, "Are we also going to Kennywood?" When I say that you can't plan everything out to perfection and have the impact be exactly what you want, this is what I mean! To be fair, Kennywood was his favorite place, and he wasn't the least bit disappointed that we were going instead to Disney, but it was a gentle, hilarious reminder that we couldn't be completely in control.

We stayed in a donated (of course) timeshare condo right on the Disney property. We rode *all* the rides in all four parks. We ate more food than anyone could possibly imagine. I remember getting the picture of us riding Expedition Everest roller coaster at Animal Kingdom, all five of us together, wide-eyed with excitement. As your eyes scale down from Trey's arms in the air to his eyes alive with joy, his body rigid with adrenaline, you notice something. His foot and leg were pointed out, dangerously close to being outside of the car and in danger of being ripped off. The reality was that we were always that close to calamity. It's no wonder that Rachel said much more often than she'd ever have liked, "Dear Lord!"

In a lot of ways, even though we got there through the most extraordinary of circumstances, this was peak normal for us. We were just a family going on a normal (extremely expensive) vacation. Trey was just a kid with cancer, not a cancer kid. Joe and Bella were part of a family going to Disney, not the siblings of a kid with a last chance, once-in-a-lifetime experience. Rachel and I were simply pushing ourselves to the point of collapsing each day like any other two parents who were there did. It was phenomenal. It was exhausting. Rachel and I could have really used a vacation to recover from all these trips. We would not be getting one any time soon.

## How To Stand

When faced with a life-threatening diagnosis, the reality is that life is on the line for everyone, not just the child with the illness. For that reason, one must take every opportunity to live life in that time. It is not easy. It is exhausting. IT IS NOT A VACATION. To expect otherwise is foolish. However, living a "normal" life as much as possible is very beneficial to the long-term emotional health of the family, and to creating memories that will stay with you even if your child does not make it.

It is also important to note that the overall health of the family can be a limiting factor. To take a trip for the sake of memories while greatly sacrificing the present-day mental and physical health of the child, siblings, and parents is not in their best interests. Frustratingly, like everything else in this entire process, there is no cut-and-dried, step-by-step, black-and-white way to go about this. You have to think, pray, and decide what is best for you at this time. Be aware of encouragements like, "You just have to!" or "You'll always regret it if you don't!" or even "How can you go away at a time like this?" Each family and each situation is different. Rely on those you trust; those who not only have your best interests in mind but also really know you and what you are capable of getting through. They are the ones you should rely upon when deciding if to go, where to go, what to do, and who should come along for support. Remember, the immediate family is who matters most, not Grandma, not Cousin Jimmy, and especially not social media.

When deciding where to go, Make-A-Wish does it right. If you qualify for a dream to come true, use it. Set your pride aside and accept the gift that it is. Allow them to bless you. I would encourage you to find something that benefits the entire family. While meeting a professional wrestler might be the best for the child with the diagnosis, it might be just another way for a sibling to feel left out and neglected. Going somewhere or doing something that everyone would benefit from while still blessing the child with the diagnosis is a better way to go.

I've said this before, but it's worth repeating. This is not an ideal situation. You will not get the ideal trip. There will be tantrums, rude people who have no clue what you are going through, and kids who don't know that your child is battling for their lives. The list goes on. Your kids will not appreciate every moment, plans will change, everyone will be exhausted, your schedule will have to change, you will face socially awkward moments, and expectations will not be met.

However, given the proper perspective, there will be moments that make it worthwhile. There will be those mental (and occasionally actual) snapshots that you will hold on to forever. It has been said that the 10 percent of the time that you enjoy your children makes up for the 90 percent of the time that you don't (I didn't say it . . . though I get it). I would say that this is true of trips during these times as well. The frustrations, setbacks, and disappointments are more numerous than the times that things go well. However, the magnitude of the good moments carries a greater weight and can have a more positive impact than that which does not go well.

I recently watched a friend of mine who attends our church go to great lengths to convert her mother's bedroom that was being used for her hospice space into a beach-themed oasis. Walking into that room to pray with this great woman of God was almost surreal. It was transformational. I really felt like I was at the beach (her mother *loved* the beach). In the event that your loved one is too sick for a trip, perhaps you or someone can transform a room (or their room) in their house to make it more special. It clearly won't compare, but so much of this is making the best out of the worst.

Lastly, and I realized this long before Trey died, one thing we did was set ourselves up for a lifetime of (potentially expensive) vacations. It would be very damaging for Joe and Bella to no longer go away and have vacations once Trey was no longer with us. We have continued that tradition, and it has served us well. It has not been inexpensive, and no one has since lined up to pay for us to go away. Of course, we never expected this kind of gift and never wanted them to be given out of feelings of obligation. If you are given the gift of a trip or vacation at *any* time throughout the trials of a life-threatening diagnosis, accept it with gratitude! Others may see an amazing opportunity to bless you after your family's time of trauma (life or death) is over.

## How To Help Them Stand

It is important to come alongside the family as they make the decision to go away. Do not be the one who says they shouldn't or can't. If they have decided to go, it is on you to encourage it and help them get there. If the opposite is true, and they have decided to put it off and not go, support that decision. If they ask you what your opinion is, IF they ask you, carefully give it, but do so with great caution. If you say not to go and then they decide to go and it ends up being a disaster, don't you dare say, "Well, I told you not to go." Selfishly and somewhat pragmatically, you also don't want to be on the record for strong advice that ends up going badly either way.

If the family has decided to go on a trip, do everything you can to make it happen. Whether it be fundraising, trip planning, or taking care of their home while they are away, be part of the process. This should always be done in accordance with their overall plan or strategy for things during these times. Fill in where the family needs you, but not where you want to be needed. Remember, it's about them and what they need. It's not about what you want and how you want to be needed.

It is also more than okay to offer the family trips or properties you already own or have special access to. We had many people reach out to us and offer their condo or vacation home. A very dear classmate of mine designed some of the coasters at Universal Studios and wanted us to go there. We ended up not being able to accept most of these very generous offers but were always blessed by the fact that people thought of us and reached out to us. Sometimes it actually is the thought that counts and has an impact.

As mentioned in the "How To Stand" section above, there is a great opportunity to love the family by helping them go on vacations after all is said and done. Not too long after their treatment is complete (or the child sadly passes away), most of the people who came alongside the family move on, hoping that the family has as well. To help fund or organize a vacation for them would be tremendously impactful.

# CHAPTER 13

# When Things Turn for the Worse

AFTER TREY'S SURGERY FAILED AND HE NEARLY DIED ON THAT OPERATING TABLE, I KNEW HIS DAYS WERE NUMBERED. Granted, I didn't know the number, but, according to his doctors and barring a miracle (more on that later), I would be seeing my son pass sooner than I should. When he was diagnosed, I knew it was a possibility. There were times throughout when my mind wandered to what that might look like. Rachel and I certainly didn't talk about it a lot, if ever. To a degree, that was my burden to bear in regard to what that time would look like, how to prepare, and how to best be ready for that which you are never supposed to experience. Now, that time was coming.

Trey's health was relatively outstanding. Granted, he had terminal cancer, but he was healthy. Yes, I am aware of how crazy that sounds. He had his regular visits to the hospital and the occasional colds and whatnot, but for the most part, he was a normal kid. We would go and get his scans and see what the cancer was doing and go about life.

With that being said, we were running out of options. There would be that horrific radiation treatment that would prolong his life some more. I say "horrific" in relation to what Trey (and actually more so Rachel) had to go through, but in reality, Trey handled it like anything else. It seemed to be no big deal. I won't go into it more than I already have, but it's one of those times where you can't believe anyone is going through this, especially you. Other than that, we could only live life and wait.

I spent many a night wondering how the end would be and what it would look like. How would I possibly take Joe and Bella into a room and have them say goodbye to Trey? What would my last words be to him? What if he died in the middle of the night and Joe (who shared a room with him) found him? Would we have to move? I didn't inherently lose sleep over it, but if I was awake in the middle of the night, this topic was certainly on my mind.

I began to make a folder of what I wanted to remember "when the time comes." I put in songs I wanted to be played at the funeral service. I would want certain things to be said and specific Scripture to be used. I felt that it helped me to be—not more prepared, but less unprepared if and when he passed . . . and then he did.

It was late October, and Trey began to wither a bit. This was nothing completely out of the ordinary, as there were many ups and downs over the years of his sickness. My sister Cathy had come to visit, as we were never sure when that time would come. Then, within a day or so, he got worse. He was still up and about. He would play, go out with us, and watch his videos. He just got tired, really tired, quickly. One night we noticed that he was in a good bit of pain and that his stomach was kind of bulging and hard. We called the physician on duty, and rather than bring him in, she said to give him more pain medication and see how he was in the morning. Rachel decided to sleep on the floor of his and Joe's bunk bed (Trey was on the bottom) just to be next to him. She had never done this before. Their last words to each other were "I love you."

The next morning, as Joe was in the bathroom getting ready for school, Rachel came to me in a quiet panic. She motioned for me to follow her to the boys' bedroom, where I saw him. He was gone. He had died in his sleep. Joe, praise God, did not notice his brother, and we brought his clothes out for him to continue getting ready for the day. I took Joe to school while Rachel got Bella ready. I raced to take her and then hurried home. Not knowing the proper protocol and procedures, we called the funeral home. When they showed up, they asked when the police had left. We hadn't called the police. We didn't know we were supposed to do that. The police came and went through the proper procedures, and then the funeral home took Trey's body.

Then . . . we cried. We cried really hard for quite some time. There's something amazing about the depths of that despair. I have never felt closer to Rachel and yet less able to make things better. Some things can't be made better; they can only be made not worse.

We made phone calls to our immediate family and went to go get Joe and Bella to tell them. We got home and made our official post on social media. I set up appointments with the funeral home and the church where we would hold the viewings and funeral service. That evening, we all gathered at my sister Mary Lynn's house, where we'd all grown up. There were tears, comfort, laughter, prayer, and discussions. We all had a "toast" with frozen blueberry waffles in honor of Trey; this was one of his favorite snacks. Life had to continue on, just like it did on Christmas Eve after he was diagnosed.

The next morning, my sister Cathy, who had felt led not to go home, joined me at the church to plan his funeral service. I assured everyone there that it would not be a long meeting, as I was prepared. I opened up the file on my phone to the folder I had been "preparing" and saw that there was one song in it. There were no Bible verses, no plans, nothing other than one song. I knew I had been preparing. In reality, it was just an intention in my mind to be prepared. How do you prepare for the death of your child? I just always kept doing whatever I could to help us Stand. I would not let us fall, crumble, or be beaten by this hideous attack. I can only hope and pray that this book helps you do the same.

It did occur to me, though, that I had spent a lot of time wondering and, at times, worrying about what would happen, how it would happen, and how we would manage "that day" when it would arrive. When it did happen, Joe and Bella were completely unaware of what had transpired until we told them. There was no hospice. There were no "goodbyes." None of the other things I had worried about took place. Rachel and I could never have been prepared for what we faced that morning, but it could have been *much* worse. Now, the next phase of this journey had begun.

# How To Stand

It is helpful for someone, even if not you, to be thinking of what will happen if "it" happens. However, it is not essential. Again, there is no ideal preparation; there is just avoiding further pain and anguish. It would have helped me if I had someone to work through some of these thoughts, ideas, and plans with for if and when that day would come. I never reached out to anyone and there wouldn't have been many people who I would have gone "there" with, but it would have helped.

A lot of what made it the "least worst" situation is the work we had put in during our journey. If we did not already have the support of our family, community, and church, this experience would have been different. We hadn't gone over what to do if he *did* die with those people, but we had those people. They knew, like us, that it was a very distinct possibility that Trey would die. Had we chosen to go it alone (as per chapter 2), this would have been even more difficult when he did. With that being said, please know that you should call the police, a funeral home that you trust, a church that you can use, and a place to have the funeral meal.

It is important to focus on the now. Be present as much as possible. Spending a lot of time thinking of and planning for the worst-case scenario is somewhat wasteful. There are so many variables in play that you are not going to be able to prepare for all of them. In doing so, you will probably miss out on many moments of opportunity and blessing.

Make sure you aren't completely alone at this time. Certainly, be alone as much as you'd like or need, but don't be completely alone. If you are completely alone, you will remember two things whenever you look back on it. First, you will hyper-focus in on the tragic and horrific loss of your child. Second, you will see that no one was there. I will always remember that beautifully horrific time Rachel and I shared. Our time with our family that evening was essential to our healing. We were surrounded by exactly the amount of family and friends that we needed. I cannot stress to you how much we were blessed by that comfort. Again, you matter most. Yet, it is also very helpful for others to be able to grieve with you. I may be unique and idealistic in that viewpoint, but it is true nonetheless.

## How To Help Them Stand

If you have (or are) someone who has experience with these types of circumstances and are very organized, you could pull the parents aside (or one of them) and say, "God forbid, if that day ever comes, I'm prepared to walk you through every step of the way. I'm here to celebrate the victory, but, God forbid, I'm also here to make the worst potentially bearable." It may be the only thing you (or they) ever offer to do for the parents, but it would be a good emotional safety net.

It is important that the parents and family not be alone too much immediately after the death of their child. They do need their space. We needed our alone time for sure. However, to be with our family the evening it happened was essential. We were able to not be alone in our suffering. We could talk about it, not talk about it, laugh, cry, and celebrate Trey's life. It wasn't easy, but it was helpful. Our family was amazing at joining us emotionally. I will forever remember that love. The next evening, Rachel's friends came over and, once again, we were not alone. It should be noted that they wanted to come over the night Trey died. We told them it wasn't necessary (or desired) and, very importantly, they listened to us. Trust them when they tell you what they want or need. We had our moments alone, but we were not left all alone. To go through what we went through and then to be left alone would have been far worse.

One could argue, though, that there is something that could be worse than being completely alone. It's when *that* person barges in. You know, the (insert obnoxious personality trait here) person. I'll even bet you just thought of someone. Don't be that person. Read the room. The hard thing is, this person rarely knows he or she is that way. If someone says to you, "Maybe you should give them some time," it may be their way of telling you that you are *that* person. Grief Share is a ministry that helps people deal with the loss of a loved one. They have an actual term for the people who barge in and think they know exactly what the grieving person needs. They're called "Invaders." They invade your space, your peace, your privacy, and even your grief. Don't be an Invader.

# CHAPTER 14

# Surviving the Worst Week of Your Life

IN AND OF ITSELF, THE TITLE OF THIS CHAPTER MAY BE MISLEADING. I titled it as such because no one ever wants to imagine, let alone think of or believe, that this could ever happen. At the beginning of Trey's treatment, I remember signing a document (I think I had to sign it, but maybe I just read it) that said, "This is a potentially terminal disease and your child may die." I sat there and stared at it thinking, *Holy crap, Trey really could die.* Clearly his death and the aftermath would constitute the worst week of my life, and in many ways, it was. However, the number of people who were there for us and joined us in our pain kept it from getting worse.

Rachel and I met with the funeral director, a fellow in our community we had known loosely for years. It was great having someone we knew, respected, and trusted to help us through this time. We picked out a casket, which, even after all we'd been through, made our stomachs drop (vomit), and we began to talk about cemeteries. He explained that we would be buying three plots, one each for Rachel, myself, and Trey. That had never occurred to me. So, I was twenty-four hours or so from my son dying and contemplating and planning for my own burial.

We are not people big on visiting cemeteries. When people die, they are gone. However, you have to be buried somewhere. It didn't make sense to bury him with Rachel's dad in the north hills of Pittsburgh (we live out east), and the main one in Penn Hills was, perhaps, too close. We weren't sure how we'd feel if we were always driving by and being reminded of all that had happened. That's when Russ (the funeral director) suggested Plum Creek Cemetery.

"It's beautiful with streams, trees, and rolling hillsides," he said.

I replied, "Wait, you want me to be buried in Plum? No way!"

He looked at me quite confused and said, "You're kidding, right?"

I cleared things up and said, "Look, I almost didn't hire you because you're not in Penn Hills; you think I want my body to spend eternity in Plum (our high school and community rival)?" So, Mt. Hope cemetery in Penn Hills it was. Remember, even in the worst moments of your life, you're still you.

As it turns out, having Trey buried so close to home was neither a stumbling block for us nor a benefit. It's not like what we went through is ever far from our minds. Driving past it does bring us the occasional tinge of sadness, but so does a picture, commercial, or fleeting thought. We've only been there one other time since Trey died, and that was to bury my father in the next plot over.

We went to meet with the man who runs the cemetery. Joe was a kind and gentle older man. It was impressive to watch him learn about us and how we prioritized things. He explained how often they mow and clear things up, and we couldn't have cared less. He then focused more on the coming days and how things would proceed. He warned us about buying a headstone from independent dealers, as they often use limestone from the South, and when those stones are placed in the North, they erode very quickly. Joe showed us examples and made us understand how things worked throughout the entire process. That information, demystifying the process of burial, more than the mowing, gave us comfort. He gave us a very generous discount given the fact that Trey was so young. Even given that, nothing could prepare us completely for the loss of our child, and the cost to bury him (the entire process, not just the cemetery) was shocking.

I mentioned Rachel's friends coming over the day after Trey died. It was the next evening (after we had planned the viewing and funeral), and their visit helped us blow off steam. Rachel doesn't see them nearly as much as she did when she was younger, so their presence was a great reminder that lifetime friends are rooted in loyalty and commitment, not necessarily geography and frequency. It was a blessing to see them that evening.

A lot of what happened in the days leading up to the viewing is a blur. We kept Joe and Bella busy with aunts, uncles, and friends through lunches and shopping, but we also made sure we had time together. We had a lot of communication with the church as to what we wanted and needed for the viewing. We decided to hold the viewing at the church, as there would probably be too little room for all those coming to pay their respects. We also needed space for the different "stations" and displays that were to celebrate what God had done through Trey's life as well as space to keep any younger ones entertained and busy.

I can't thank Carrie Hendrickson and her team from the church enough. We put an awful lot on her plate for the viewings. We had an area where you could write your favorite memories of Trey, a board where you could sign your name if you were one of Trey's "girlfriends," a place where you could tell us how God used this time to reach you through our tragedy, and other stations as well. We wanted a room for the kids where they could watch videos, do crafts, and be away (as much as possible) from the awkwardness. The church also provided a private family room where we could take a break or meet with everyone before and after the viewings. Carrie made sure everything was as we had asked it to be.

I had tried to imagine what these days would look like for me and for Rachel, but I couldn't have begun to imagine what the experience would be like for Bella and Joe. I assigned another adult to each of them who would be their primary caregiver during the viewings. It would be too lofty of a goal to think that Rachel and I could hug five hundred people, talk with people we hadn't seen in years, mourn the death of our son, and still properly attend to all of Joe's and Bella's needs. Rather, each of them had their own person who they already knew and loved directly watching over and engaging with them. Having someone to walk them through this time was much more ideal. The kids called the shots. You want to be in the main room? Great. You want to do a craft? Awesome. You want to hang out with the other kids who are there? You can do that. I even gave them the option to just up and leave and go to McDonald's if they wanted. Joe and Bella had experienced so much that was out of their control that I had to give them some semblance of authority over their own lives.

Then, the day of the first viewing came. We had decided to do afternoon and evening times of 2:00 p.m.–4:00 p.m. and 6:00 p.m.–8:00 p.m. the first day and then straight 3:00 p.m.–8:00 p.m. (big mistake) the second. We had people watching our house during the visitations, for we had heard that thieves will look at obituaries and rob the houses during the visitation. Isn't that something? As we were pulling out, our dear neighbor from across the street came running out. She hadn't heard about Trey until just then. She was sobbing and so sorry for us. Her emotion was so kind and thoughtful, but she was also keeping us from being on time for the viewing. She realized that and let us go. It would not be the last time where someone was grieving differently than we were. It's an odd thing to get used to.

We walked into the hall where the viewing was taking place, and it was as perfect as your son's viewing could be. There was the picture of Trey on top of the casket, and that picture perfectly portrayed who he was. Bella just asked me the other day why we went with a closed casket (eight-plus years later). I told her that we (though it was Rachel's thoughtful idea) wanted to remember him for who he was alive and not in his death. Having an open casket is often important so that people get closure, but how could you ever really get closure with the death of a six-year-old? Having it open would do more harm than good, we decided.

Then, people started coming in. As expected, a lot of people showed up. We had decided to make a dedicated queue for people to follow those stations along the way. There needed to be order in the chaos. For the most part, I had two people (typically my sisters) next to me as I greeted people. As we talked with those who came to pay their respects, I would introduce them to one of my sisters. All the while, my inner monologue was constantly spinning and being hypervigilant. Even though I had people taking care of Bella and Joe, I was still monitoring how they were doing as well as how we were doing. I was purposeful in making sure Rachel was okay. I wanted us to properly grieve but quickly realized that, as odd as it seems, this wasn't the time for that.

I apologize right now to all the people who I don't mention in the following segment. There are many that I simply don't remember due to the numbers and overwhelming nature of the time. However, several people stood out for different reasons. Two people made me lose it when I saw them. One was Joe Hines, an elderly man who was on my Young Life committee. He was just a father figure to me, and the running joke was that he *was* Rachel's father. We sometimes told the Young Life kids that for fun, and that was hilarious in that he is African American. Just seeing him there made me feel loved and cared for. The second was Mr. Thompson, the man who was both my fourth and sixth grade teacher . . . I was lucky enough to have him twice. When I saw Mr. Thompson, I sobbed. I had loosely kept in contact with him over the years. He was the strict, "no nonsense" type of teacher who you maybe didn't like when you were a student but appreciated more over time. Now, here he was paying his respects to me for a test of faith and endurance he had (unknowingly) prepared for me to take.

My friend Butch stood there in line. It was an emotional experience to see someone far back in the line but having to wait forty-five minutes to even make it to where Rachel and I were standing. Butch had driven to the viewing from his home in Virginia. He paid his respects and drove home. That's loyalty.

Some of the strongest men I knew cried the hardest. One man in particular I'd known for a long time but not very well. Bob Martini is the physical fitness coach at the high school. He waited in line for the entire time, but when he got to us, he was overwhelmed with sadness. He tried to speak but couldn't. He tried again but continued to cry, so he excused himself and left. Moments later, I saw him again . . . back in line. It was thirty or so minutes more before he made his way back to us.

"Jay and Rachel, I apologize for how I acted earlier. I am so sorry for your loss."

I smiled and looked at him, reassuring him by saying, "Bob, what you did earlier was the best. You showed us how much you cared. You just wasted forty minutes of your life to come up here and try to tell us. We already knew." We all laughed and he went away in a much better place. The viewing was filled with moments like that with people we didn't expect.

Another example of unexpected connection was with my brother's longtime friend and business partner, Bill. Rather than wait in the line to say the stereotypical condolences, he skipped the line to get within fifteen feet or so of us. He and I made eye contact. He put his hand up, bowed his head down, and nodded. I gave him the same head nod back and he left. It was perfect. He didn't want to waste anyone's time and just wanted us to know that he was there and cared. I know he was there for my brother as much as or more than me. It was great.

I also remember one poor lady who showed up in a fur(ish) coat. It had been raining, and she definitely had a lot of cats. She hugged me and held on dearly, my face buried in her fur (the coat and the cat's). It was wet, cold, and not pleasing to the nose (I'm allergic to cats). I also remember that my face was beginning to feel . . . raw. I then realized I had hugged so many men with beards that I was slowly getting a brush burn on my cheek. At no point in our journey with Trey did I expect something like this to happen.

I remember Rachel's high school friend Todd being there . . . a lot. He was a county police officer and was technically on duty. I guess he had to be somewhere in the county, so he chose to be there. He ran errands for us and was generally available. Nice surprises like that were a-plenty in those two days and were all aspects I didn't plan for, but God provided.

Before the viewing on the second day, my family came out of the private room, and I saw my brother by himself looking at the picture of Trey above the casket. He turned and looked at me and began to cry. You have to understand. Tommy and I are men. Further, we are Mitlo men. We are in control. We are the helpers. In this moment, we were both sad, but we weren't alone. It was a beautiful moment where we cried, hugged, looked at each other, laughed, and got ready for everyone to come in.

I mentioned earlier that the second day's long five-hour visitation span was a mistake, and it was. I don't remember why we chose to do it that way. I mean, we were both adding an hour and removing a break, neither of which would help us endure the emotions before us. I recall Rachel having a reason for it, but looking back, we both wish we had done that differently. I suppose it was still a blessing because when it was over, we were done. Emotionally, relationally, and physically . . . we were spent. We certainly don't think we should have or could have done more.

The next morning was the funeral.

I remember nothing of that morning before the funeral. We gathered in the "family room" of the church, and there was some general nervousness and commotion but nothing out of the ordinary or noteworthy. Then, I realized something. I was standing in a room with my parents, my brother and sisters, my closest friends, Rachel, Joe, and Bella. Everyone was waiting for me. No one was taking the lead. It was up to me. It was daunting and yet affirming to take this last step out in faith and lead everyone in this moment as I had been doing now for years. I had earned that right throughout this whole process.

I noticed something else as I began to speak with all of them. My guys were standing in the back of the room. Who were "my guys"? They were my brothers in Christ, the people I had led with in Young Life, men who had come to know Christ through my years in ministry, some of my closest friends, and even some I hadn't seen very much lately at all. They were all there. They said nothing. They did nothing. After all, there was nothing they could do or say. They were simply there in support of me. Looking back, they will never know how much that meant to me and what it did for me as we went out for the funeral service for my son. Seeing all this true and earnest support was easily one of the top three most impactful moments of my life.

I prayed, and we headed out to the sanctuary for the service. I led the way boldly, knowing what had to be done. The day we all feared could come was here, and we had to get through it. However, I was bound and determined not just to get through it but to see it through. God had allowed this horrific time for a reason, and I was not going to miss His purpose in this.

We sang worship songs that praised God and vowed our commitment to Him, despite our sorrowful condition. I don't remember the number of songs or if anything else was said before it was my time to speak. I took the stage and looked at the crowd. Nothing can quite prepare you for that moment. It was absolutely overwhelming to see the wide array of people in attendance. It was almost confusing to see people from so many different aspects of our lives all in one room, all there to love and support us. I actually began my eulogy by taking pictures of those in attendance. I'm sure no one wanted their tear-stained faces captured at that moment, but I wanted to be able to look back and remember who was there. I treasure those pictures.

I've never gone back to listen to my eulogy for my son, but I have heard from many the impact it had on them. I do remember that my main points were as follows:

No one thought that Trey was all that special before he had cancer.

No one said that Rachel and I were such faithful people before Trey was diagnosed.

**Out of respect for Rachel, I need to point out that, yes, we were known as people *of faith*. Sure. However, we were not known specifically or especially for our faithfulness. We were known as loving, funny, energetic people who loved to reach out to high school kids.**

The point is, we are now known as faithful people because we have endured what no one could imagine having to go through. Trey became inspirational through his ordeal and resolve.

Joe and Bella were revered as resilient through this unspeakable time. What was important was not who we were before, but what God provided to, in, and through us when needed. God could have spared us from all of this but loved everyone so much that He gave them this demonstration of provision, power, and compassion.

If God was not to be glorified in all of this, then it was simply a tragedy and an innocent life lost. We knew that God was to be glorified and we did so.

I remember walking off the stage, specifically stepping down from the very last step, and thinking, *I did it. I passed the test. I graduated. What the enemy chose to destroy me didn't work. I held strong and faithful and used it for good.* I and my family were able to Stand when the day of evil approached.

The service ended as they began to play "10,000 Reasons" by Matt Redman. The music played as we, as a family, walked with the casket out of the building. I looked back at Barrett, leading worship, and nodded. He belted out the first line of the song and the people began to sing. I will always appreciate that last moment of solidarity and support. He knew what I wanted, he understood my communication, and everyone was led to worship.

We went to the cemetery, where there was a quick service in the chapel. I remember none of it. We went to eat. I remember next to none of it. We went home. I have no idea what the rest of the day looked like. It was over. Well, that part of the battle and journey was over. The next one had just begun.

## How To Stand

Before I say anything else, know this. You can get through this. When all else fails . . . Stand. You don't have to win, advance, or even make any progress. Just Stand in the face of evil's greatest attack and make it another minute, hour, and day. You can get through this. You are stronger than you would ever imagine.

Below is an outline I have used to help other people who have gone through this horrific time. I believe that they can help you or someone you love who is going through this.

# Personally

- Be open, honest, and vulnerable—be as present in all things as possible. Being present may mean that you must allow yourself and others to be sad, angry, quiet, or even sobbing.

- As I have already mentioned earlier, this is a time when you can—and perhaps should—be selfish. You and your immediate family come first. If you want people around, fine. If not, fine. You don't have to say yes to anything. You don't have to organize or accommodate anyone.

- Feel free to do any or all of the following if you like, but remember that you are in charge. Get rest, eat, sleep, shop, exercise, stay home, go out, or work. Say no . . . a lot if need be.

# Emotionally

- Give yourself grace (you can't do this perfectly). That grace can allow you to realize that we all grieve differently and at different times. It's perfectly normal to feel nothing for extended periods of time. It's okay if you lose it in sadness or anger; minimize the exposure and damage. Talk as much as you can; encourage (but don't force) the same. Remember that while others may have it worse or gone done a similar path, your pain is yours, and it's incredibly and horrifically unique.

- Realize that you will feel pain for others in this process. It's hard to watch anyone grieve. Just because they are grieving for you doesn't make it hurt less. In a weird way, you are only grieving once (in a HUGE way) as you are grieving the loss of your child. Others are grieving for the loss of their grandson, niece, neighbor, etc., while also grieving for you and *your* loss. It's a weird thing.

# Practically

- Do not do this alone; be as organized as you can be. Have a right-hand man/woman for each of you. They will know all the details of the events of the week. They will know who's responsible for each event, meal, or service. This right-hand man or woman will check in with you but not depend on you to do everything. They can make decisions when you cannot.

- Get a meal train program up immediately. Sifting through five hundred lasagnas and casseroles gets old quick. Be specific about likes, dislikes, and allergies.

If you're doing a viewing(s), then keep them to the two or three-hour segments. Having two in one day is okay if they are separated by a break.

- Make sure you have good queue management. Consider setting up stations for different categories of the child's life (outside of the queue/line). You can put pictures or memorabilia at each one. This will help people find each other and grieve together. This will also help keep areas from clogging. Have at least two people with you at the front. They can take the people who want to talk too long. They can also get you whatever you need.

- You'll probably have a private room in the building. Use this space to prepare your closest loved ones before you go out. Make it (have someone make it) as comfortable as possible.

- If there will be kids (under ten) attending, then have places and activities for them. This can be weird and scary but also a time for them to ask questions and feel loved.

- Set up people (or have your right-hand man/woman do it) to take care of your daily tasks. Cutting the grass, shopping, cleaning, or even paying bills will not be tasks you can focus on in this difficult time. This can go on for as long as you'd like or need.

- Caring for your immediate family is a practical concern as well. Have someone dedicated to caring for the siblings. If they need to leave a viewing or family gathering, they should be able to. They have experienced the worst thing yet in their lives. They have experienced something that (hopefully) no one they know has gone through. They have learned that they have NO control. Allowing them some control in these days will be instrumental in their grieving and healing. Yes, they are your children, but you'll be distracted and grieving on your own. Others will be honored to focus on them. They will appreciate (perhaps) the specific attention to their present needs as compared to their horrific loss. Give your surviving children every opportunity to tell their story. What they have experienced (are experiencing/will continue to experience) is different than anyone else. They may not want to talk about the loss and it shouldn't be forced, but it should be available to happen organically. When it's over, get them out of there. Don't linger.

- You and your spouse should be together as much as possible. That's a given but needs to be pointed out. Cry together (I'm sure that's been done). Make sure, especially this week, to check in on how the week is going as well as checking in purposefully on the overall devastation you are experiencing. The two of you are one in God's eyes. The enemy will use this time to drive a wedge in between you. Don't allow that.

- It's okay to laugh when things are funny. It's okay to laugh when things are just too awkward. It's okay to cry at all times. It's very okay to just be quiet.

- With that being said, surround yourselves with your closest of friends. Make sure your spouse's friends know exactly what they need. Keep them up to date with how your spouse is doing. Use these friends to help protect your spouse from annoying relatives, coworkers, or neighbors; putting too much pressure on himself or herself; pushing too hard, or being too perfect. Make sure you have at least one or two friends with whom you can be really real.

- In regard to the funeral, yes, the goal is to get through it. However, don't miss the opportunity for very real and powerful moments. It's the funeral of your child. You get to make the calls. Customize it to be as real and intimate as possible. Do as much as you'd like or as little as you'd need.

## How To Help Them Stand

- As someone close to the family . . .
  - Step up to do anything that is asked of you.
    - Be on point to coordinate any or every service.
    - Lead a project like picture boards, stations/areas of the viewing, refreshments, meals at the viewing/ funeral, meal train, greeters at the door, helping with the kids, etc.
  - Gently offer to do things that were not asked.
    - If the parents have missed something, offer to step in.
    - These could be but are not limited to . . . household necessities, store runs, or simply checking in with them every half hour to see if they're okay or need a break.

- o Be available. It is good knowing that a trusted loved one is there and ready to help at a moment's notice.

- As someone further away but still wanting to help . . .
  - o Do the selfless things.
    - Watch their house during services (thieves actually look up obituaries and target those homes . . . disgusting).
    - Help with setup and cleanup.
    - Talk with people who seem to be alone (this takes a special skill set).
    - Help the helpers by checking in with them and seeing if they need anything.
  - o Be a "model" for others to follow (more on that in the next section).
    - Find out how things are supposed to run.
      - Make sure the guest book is where people can find it.
      - Set up one or more of the stations (pictures, stories, videos).
      - Take charge of the signup for the post funeral dinner.
    - Help guide others to follow the intended flow.

# General Funeral Guidelines

The sad truth about viewings and funerals is that you don't get to talk to the people you'd like to talk to nearly enough and you have to talk to people you don't want to talk to at all. Viewings and funerals are emotional minefields. Ironically, it is very often those around the grieving family who explode while those grieving the hardest are too emotionally numb to react. Be careful not to be too high or too low in your demeanor. You don't want to appear to be too happy and indifferent nor the saddest person there. Please remember, while you are grieving, it's not about you. There's a reason why for years it's been "paying your respects." "Paying" connotes that it costs you something—your comfort, your time, your attention. "Respects" connotes an attitude reflecting a focus on others rather than yourself.

Know this: less is more. I don't remember one good thing someone said to me throughout Trey's viewing or funeral. I do remember awkward moments. I don't remember one encouraging word or Scripture verse shared. I do remember having to comfort those who were actively and outwardly grieving harder than I was in the moment.

Here's what had the greatest impact on me. People were there. Who showed up mattered much more than what they said. I mentioned my brother's former business partner in this chapter. He was perfect and never said a word. I also mentioned "my guys." I'm not sure if one of them ever spoke. Their faces standing in the back of the room will forever be etched in my mind.

If I were to be brutally honest, speaking as the father of a child who died and as a pastor who has participated in many funerals, there are several categories of people in attendance at viewings and funerals . . .

1. People who you expect to be there, and you're glad they came

2. People who you expect to be there, but you have to endure

3. People who you expect to be there, but they didn't show up

4. People who you didn't expect to be there, and you're really moved that they came

The real opportunity to be a blessing lies in #4. I once made someone feel incredibly loved when I showed up for less than two minutes at a viewing for the very elderly mother of a person I only professionally know. I didn't even speak with them.

Here are four ways people make mistakes at viewings and funerals when talking with those who are grieving.

1. Ignoring—they ignore what those grieving are feeling. They just chit-chat or make nervous banter.

2. Being selfish—they "steal their story" by sharing their loss. This also happens when they grieve (at the moment) more than those they came to see.

3. Being critical—this is rarely on purpose (that would be horrific) but happens a lot. These are things like saying,

"Don't cry" or giving them Bible verses that speak about hope, joy, or healing. While true, they connote that what those grieving are feeling is wrong.

4. Speaking "truth"—"He's in a better place," "Everything happens for a reason," "He's with Jesus now," "He's no longer suffering," and "God has a plan" are all examples of true statements that (like #1) are ignoring their pain.

Rather, and pardon me for being a pastor and stating the obvious, you should be more like Jesus. In John 11, Jesus knew He was going to heal Lazurus. However, remember what He did as He came upon Mary and Martha (Lazarus's sisters) crying . . . He wept. He joined them in their emotions.

Notice (given the list above) what He didn't do.

1. He did not walk right past them.

2. He did not tell them how much it broke His heart to have to let Lazurus die while waiting to heal him to show how great His Father was.

3. He did not tell them that they lacked faith.

4. He did not explain what He was doing, that Lazurus was going to be fine, and that this would be written about for people to see forever.

They would forever remember the day that Jesus wept with them (and that He healed their brother). That's how comfort works. You certainly remember the pain, but someone being there (emotionally) with you is then attached to that pain. Comfort is attached and heals the grief.

CHAPTER 15

# What About Miracles?

MANY PEOPLE TOLD US FROM DAY ONE OF TREY'S DIAGNOSIS THAT THEY BELIEVED IN MIRACLES. We asked for, solicited, and coveted the prayers of many . . . pretty much from any who would spend time before God on our behalf.

Early on, I had the idea to keep a map of each place where someone was praying for us. I thought it would be a good way for Joe and Bella to realize how amazing the people of God are and learn a little bit about geography.

We went so far as to get a map of the United States and planned to put thumbtacks where people were praying. We may have even done that for a minute or two. However, a few things precluded us from continuing to do that. One, the area of those who were praying became much bigger than just the United States, and we couldn't get enough maps! Two, there were just so many to keep up with it. Finally, three, we just had too much to do to keep up with it.

I mentioned my man Amol in chapter 3. What a blessing he was and is (we keep in touch to this day). Back then, he assured me that the widows and orphans of his ministries would be praying for Trey every Thursday. I remember wondering how many sick children there were between India and Penn Hills for which these people could be praying. Yet, they were praying for my boy.

Shortly thereafter, I received a message from a woman who ran an orphanage in the Philippines. She told me that her "twenty-four children of light" would be lifting Trey up in prayer. One person told me that they stuck a prayer on a note and placed it in the Wailing Wall of Jerusalem. People were praying for us from all over the world. Not just people in our small Pennsylvania community, but widows, orphans, and missionaries from around the world.

Back home, we had a weekly "Pray for Trey" group. Wherever you were, at 9:00 p.m. on Tuesdays, our friend Christina would post a reminder (and perhaps a focus) for prayer. My sister Cathy began to write a weekly devotional specifically for Trey and our family. Thousands of people joined in and interceded on our behalf to God.

At certain times and in dire moments, people dropped everything to pray. When Trey almost died on the operating table, a church that had passed on me being their pastor held a prayer vigil. I will always remember Mr. Doyle telling me,

"When you can no longer Stand, know that I am kneeling, praying beside you."

When Trey's health was quickly declining just before he died, many prayer requests went out, and many people told me they were praying. Then, he passed.

So, you might say we didn't get our miracle. You might say we didn't do enough or we didn't believe enough. You would be very wrong.

Here's a partial list of the miracles we did get.

1. Trey never knew what cancer was.

2. Trey never knew he was sick.

3. Trey never knew he was dying.

4. Trey died peacefully in his sleep after saying, "I love you" to Rachel.

5. Joe and Bella did not find him after he had passed.

6. Joe and Bella made it through all of this.

7. Rachel and I became stronger through this, in our marriage and in our faith.

# How To Stand

We prayed for miracles. Most people would say we didn't get our miracle. Maybe we didn't pray hard enough. Maybe we didn't believe enough. Maybe God was punishing us. Maybe we weren't good enough people. Maybe God isn't real.

Do you see how quickly that whole thing can deteriorate? Can you see how your mind can spin and take you to dark places? I will tell you this—the enemy is trying to discourage and separate you from God this entire time. You will be tempted to base your relationship with God on His performance for you. You will be enticed to make your belief in Him contingent upon the health and well-being of your loved one.

It's not just your overall faith that is on the line. It is your day-to-day demeanor and quality of life. Bitterness is always lurking, ready to devour even your best intentions and the ones of those around you. Jealousy is ready to pounce as you see others taking the health of their family for granted. Rage is always an option when things don't go your way. Anxiety is waiting for you to have to make a decision or contemplate your future. Depression is always willing to replace hope, whether it be your outlook on the long term or the next five minutes. What about fear? Fear is persistent and relentless.

Philippians 4:6–7 tells us, "Do not be anxious about anything, but in every situation, by prayer and petition, with thanksgiving, present your requests to God. And the peace of God, which transcends all understanding, will guard your hearts and your minds in Christ Jesus." This is the way to go. However, too often people read and follow this direct instruction and then feel anxious anyhow. Then, they feel like a "bad Christian" for feeling that way. Then, when their prayer for a miracle comes back with a "no" from God, they feel like they've failed. They feel like they didn't have enough faith. They feel like they've let themselves down, they've let their loved ones down, and they've disappointed God. Do you see how dangerous this is?

It should be noted that there are two words that are almost always overlooked in those verses . . . "with thanksgiving." The same part of your brain that experiences anxiety is the same part that is engaged when you are grateful. It is physically impossible to be simultaneously grateful and anxious. The key to not being anxious is to focus instead on that for which you are grateful. That can be tremendously difficult in these times for sure. However, it doesn't change the fact that it is true.

Speaking of focus, continue on and read just the next couple of verses. Philippians 4:8–9 gives us what to think about instead! "Finally, brothers and sisters, whatever is true, whatever is noble, whatever is right, whatever is pure, whatever is lovely, whatever is admirable—if anything is excellent or praiseworthy—think about such things. Whatever you have learned or received or heard from me, or seen in me—put it into practice. And the God of peace will be with you."

It's that peace (and the giving of thanks in verse 6) that makes the difference. As you go through this process, give thanks that you know and can approach God in prayer. Give thanks that you've been blessed with the loved one in the first place. In all things, give thanks. Then, follow the directives in verses 8–9. Focus on what God IS doing. Where has He blessed you? What has He saved you from experiencing? Look for the good, and you will find it. Only focus on the bad, and you will slip into dangerous emotional places. God is good. He just doesn't do what we want Him to do all the time.

# How to Help Them Stand

I talk a lot about joining someone in their emotions. I do that because we are called to do that in Romans 12:15. "Rejoice with those who rejoice; *mourn with those who mourn.*" Emphasis has been added there for obvious reasons. Further, as pointed out in the last chapter, Jesus modeled that with Mary and Martha. However, if someone is blaming themselves for "not having enough faith," should you join them in that? The obvious answer is no, but the subtlety lies in the proper way to do that.

Rather than saying, "Stop that; you know that's not true! You're only beating yourself up!" You should say something like, "My heart is so heavy right now. I love you so much. We did everything we could, didn't we? Whatever you're feeling, I'm here with you." Why should you say that? Many reasons. The first is that I can imagine that is exactly what Jesus would say. Second, notice that you say "we" did everything; you're taking the "blame" off of them. Third, you say you are with them, and they are not alone. Lastly, you tell them you are with them in whatever they are feeling, not inherently in what they are thinking.

They've only begun the grieving process. They are in for a brutal season of life. What you say and do here cannot make them all better. It is better to be the stable, calm presence that will enable them to climb out of the dense fog of grief that has engulfed them. Your goal was to help them Stand, and you've done just that. However, they have many more attacks to Stand against. Do your best to set yourself up to be there for them in all of it.

# CHAPTER 16

# So Now What?

What happened next? What happens after this battle is "over?" There's always another battle. Well, we began to grieve. We took the entire family to a place called the Highmark Caring Place. It was perfectly suited for us, as there are small groups dedicated to different ages of kids and a separate group for parents. They further divide the parent groups into the types of loss: parents who lost a spouse, parents who lost a parent, and parents who lost a child.

The experience at the Caring Place was great for Bella. She dove right in. She made friends, did all the art projects, and was able to really begin to heal. Joe didn't feel the same way at all. He didn't have a bad experience but didn't really want to be there and didn't engage much. We offered fast food after every session and he obliged. People grieve differently from each other and so do kids. For Rachel and me, it was somewhat sideways. For the first time in many sessions, they didn't have any other parents who had lost a child. So, Rachel and I were in a group of . . . us. I suppose it worked out okay, but we were mostly there for the kids anyhow.

We resumed life and continued to heal. Joe and Bella went back to school shortly after the funeral. Joe continued his jiu-jitsu and Bella kept hanging out with Becky, Jane, and friends of her own age. We still went on vacations, and we never stopped talking about Trey. We didn't stay stuck in our grief or mourning his death, but rather celebrated his life. Rachel had pillows made from all of Trey's t-shirts and gave them to the cousins. We got together with our entire extended family on the first anniversary of Trey's passing and talked about the days before and after Trey died. Everyone's story was different, and it was so impactful to hear each one (and healthy for them to tell it).

Joe and Bella continued on through school and excelled. Bella joined a baton-twirling team, and Joe advanced to the adult classes in jiu-jitsu before he quit to play golf and volleyball throughout high school. Bella had the lead in the high school musical for her junior and senior years. They are both in college now.

The lesson they both learned is that you can experience the worst that life has to offer and survive. Many people live in fear for their entire lives in dread of something like this happening to them. Many others live in fear after they have endured something like this. Joe and Bella have learned this lesson and used it to make themselves stronger. Has it left its marks on them? Sure. Joe and Bella have both struggled with anxiety to some degree, but it hasn't stopped them. When other things knock their classmates down, Joe and Bella seem less fazed by it.

Rachel and I are closer than ever. So many couples go through something like this and divorce. We had been prepared to withstand it. Rachel is the strongest woman I know (both emotionally and physically). She works full-time now with three-year-olds at the Western Pennsylvania School for the Deaf. She gets to love and support kids who have many challenges along with hearing loss.

Me? I'm constantly frustrated at not being able to help more people (hence this book). I understand but wish people gave God more credit and me less . . . but I get why they do that. I suppose the lesson I've learned in all of this is that all we have is today. Nothing is guaranteed, but at the same time, nothing is to be feared. After all, when everything comes at me, all I have to do is Stand.

# CHAPTER 17

# After You Have Done Everything, Stand

## For Those Helping Them Stand

IF YOU HAVE READ THIS BOOK BECAUSE YOU WANTED TO HELP SOMEONE FACE THE GREATEST CHALLENGE THEIR FAMILY HAS EVER FACED, I AM WITH YOU. As I edited this book, I was challenged to address all the folks who would like to help. In that time of prayer and focus, I realized that very often, people just don't help. Some are scared that they might offend or get in the way. Others are just not sure what to do, and that is part of why I wrote this book. Some just can't begin to fathom what this family is going through and can't bring themselves to face what this poor family is experiencing. So, kudos to you for being willing to even entertain the idea of coming alongside them and helping them to survive.

However, the truth remains, while most everyone is well intentioned, not everyone is well equipped. The enemy is at work trying to wreak as much havoc as possible. Yes, a life . . . a beautiful and precious life is on the line. That attack is quite obvious. We also have very little control over that. However, that is not the only attack. A marriage is on the line. The future of the siblings hangs in the balance. People's walk with Christ (if they have one) can be greatly impacted (either way). The mental, emotional, spiritual, and even physical health of the family is at risk. Here is where we have the most ability to fight the enemy and where you are so very vital.

You see, the enemy works in the subtleties. No one goes into helping and tries to hurt, sabotage, and destroy. No one other than the enemy, of course. He very often takes the best of intentions and turns them into irrevocable hurts. Matthew 10:16 says to "be as shrewd as snakes and as innocent as doves." That is my prayer for you. May you have wisdom and discernment as you go. May you know exactly what the Lord is leading you to do. I pray that you hear the gentle whisper of the Holy Spirit telling you to go, to stop, to pray, to do, to comfort, to grieve, or to join them in their pain and celebrations.

Be aware of what the enemy is doing, but understand that Jesus is far and above more powerful and, in fact, in control. You will draw nearer to Him as you love and serve this family. I commend you for your desire to represent Him to a family that needs Him and you so very much.

# For Those Who Have Been Called To Stand

There are few words. You've been through or are going through something you never imagined would come upon you. I can only tell you this—you can experience the worst that life has to offer and . . . be okay. You do not have to allow this to end you, your marriage, your family, your dreams, or your future. I hope and pray that you seek and find your strength in Him. God always provides good with the bad. There is light in the midst of darkness. The enemy would have you believe that there is no hope and no future. The enemy is a liar. He comes to steal, kill, and destroy. Jesus has come that you may have life and life to the fullest (John 10:10). I have experienced both of these to be true. The enemy did take our son. However, God showed us that He is good. Our son is with Him. Trey lived a life of greater impact than some who live to be a hundred. We were blessed by so many people and have been provided with more love and care than we could have ever imagined. Don't let the attack cause you to miss the blessing. Don't allow the pain to prevent the healing.

I am with you. I am grieving alongside you. I am crying with and for you. I am celebrating when you celebrate. You are not alone. Countless others have walked a path similar to yours, though this journey is unique to you. This is a battle that you need God to be able to Stand. He is with you. I Stand with you.

# Appendix

# What Does It Mean To Be Alone?

Rachel and I were taught this at the Center for Relational Care and realized it during what I call the "Trey Days". We learned what love can really look like. In its simplest form, love is meeting someone's needs. If you say you love them but leave them wanting, do you really love them? But what are the needs we can meet? We all have physical, intellectual, and spiritual needs. However, we also have emotional needs. Those first three needs can be met in many different ways. Very often the "church" is good at meeting these needs. We're good at making lasagna and raising money (physical needs). We are quick to offer perspective or share our experiences (intellectual needs). We love to pray for people and point them to Christ while sharing poignant Scripture verses (spiritual needs). However, everyone (not just the church) knows very little about emotional needs and very often fails to meet them. Whereas physical, intellectual, and spiritual needs are met in a variety of fashions, emotional needs are only met within a relationship. Sadly, many people, or even most people, feel alone even within their relationships. The reason why they feel alone is that their emotional needs are not being met. Very often you hear or think the phrase "That hurt my feelings." A hurt is an emotional need not met or taken from you. If you have a need for comfort and someone tells you why you are sad, they didn't meet your need. If you have a need for security and your loved one is diagnosed with a life-threatening disease, that need for security was taken from you. Either way, when your emotional needs are not met, you feel alone. Being alone is the very worst thing that there is. Billionaires are lonely when they have no one with whom to share their wealth. Solitary confinement is the worst type of prison time one can do. Yes, a little alone time is refreshing from time to time, but beyond that, it is torture. Being alone is actually the first problem God encountered here on earth.

Go back to the beginning. I mean the very beginning. God created the heavens and the earth, and it was good. Then He created everything in and about the earth, and it was good. Then He created the animals, birds, and creatures of the sea, and it was good. Then He created Adam, and it was *not* good. It was not good because Adam was alone. Don't read your Bible too quickly. What did Adam have going for him? He was in the most beautiful and plentiful place on earth (a nice, comfortable place to live). His job was naming all of God's creatures (easy job). He was the most advanced of all creations (status). Finally, he had a walking and talking relationship with the God of all creation (spiritual fulfillment). He had EVERYTHING we yearn for in our world today. Even though he had all that man could ever want, he was alone. What happens next is crucial to understanding the point I'm making (and have made throughout this book). God did not fix this problem with more of Himself. He did not say, "I should spend more time with Adam; he seems lonely." When I hear the fairly typical Christian response to being lonely, "I have my Jesus and that's all I need," I want to ask them if they think they are better than Adam was before sin entered the world. You see, God didn't give Adam more of Himself. God didn't spend more time with him. God created a relationship. He created Eve. Then, it was not only good; it was very good.

That is, until sin entered the world. Sin came in through an attack on all that was good by the enemy (Satan). You are reading this book because the enemy has attacked once again. Whether it be your son or daughter who has been diagnosed, or you are loving someone who is going through this, understanding how to love them is vital to Standing in the face of this attack. People will come alongside suffering parents and offer physical, intellectual, and spiritual needs by the boatful. However, very few—if any—people will meet their emotional needs.

Romans 12:15 says to "rejoice with those who rejoice and mourn with those who mourn." That is joining someone in their emotions and stopping them from feeling alone. It is the very definition of comfort. Look at what it isn't. It's not telling them not to be sad. It's not giving them a new perspective on their situation. It's not pointing out how good God is despite this current trial or tribulation. Jesus Himself modeled this in John 11:35 when He wept with Mary and Martha. He did not tell them that they lacked faith. He didn't assure them that He was about to heal them. He wept with them. They would forever remember the day that Jesus not only healed their brother but took the time and emotional energy to weep with them. I guarantee you that they did not feel alone in that moment.

When you join someone in their emotions, they no longer feel alone. You are, in that moment, doing exactly what God intended in the garden of Eden. You are loving them. You are attaching comfort to their grief. When Rachel and I learned all about this, it enabled us to survive the greatest challenge of our lives. It enabled us to Stand.

# Resources for Those Standing

If you search for resources on how to survive this attack, you may be overwhelmed by the many different organizations, ministries, and agencies that offer a wide array of assistance to families going through something like this. This could be another way for someone to help take the lead in helping you get through this. Researching the best resources for your family may be the very assistance you need. For us, two places were instrumental in getting us through this time.

## The Center for Relational Care.

Website: relationalcare.org

Phone: (512) 492-6200

Email: info@relationalcare.org

This is where we were trained in emotional needs and responding. I corresponded with them throughout the Trey

Days. We went there in the months after Trey died to further our knowledge and understanding of grief and comfort.

## The Highmark Caring Place

Website: highmarkcaringplace.com

Phone: (888) 224-4673

They have an amazing program to help the entire family begin to deal with grief. It is tailored for both the kids and the parents while supporting the entire family as a whole.

While it did not exist during our battle, I would also highly recommend . . .

## Pressing On

Website: pressingon.org

Email: info@pressingon.org

This organization was started by the Reeder family, who watched us go through all of this and then had their own battle and opportunity to Stand. Realizing the great chasm between social work and the chaplains at the hospital, they work to come alongside families at children's hospitals and equip them as best they can.

In general, my best advice is to talk to people (or have someone do that for you). I wouldn't inherently use online reviews but rather reach out to the social workers at the hospital and have a very open and frank conversation about what you need (if you even know what that is). Talk to others who have gone down this road and see what they have found to work. This can also be a very valuable thing that a church can do. As a church, vet the resources in the area so that when the time comes, they are ready to offer real assistance.

# Testimonies To Our Standing[1]

When I first heard about Trey, it was when they were looking for people to help with the spaghetti dinner. I don't know exactly why, but as I listened to a very brief description of who you were, it grabbed me. I mean really grabbed. If that wasn't the Holy Spirit smacking me in the face . . . I don't know what it was. Whatever it was, I was there. I wanted to help. I wanted to be the person who got things done. I wanted to be the game changer. (I know, dorky. But, alas this is what you get with me.)

I was able to get donations of food, and me and my family spent quite a few hours boiling spaghetti noodles. The more I met with the group who was running the dinner and listened to your family talk about you and Rachel and Trey and his situation . . . I was so moved. I can't even explain to you what was happening in my heart, my soul. I have had experiences where, you know, you just feel the presence of God. I mean you just FEEL it. I lost that for a while and this . . . terrible situation . . . brought me back. I put all I had into that fundraiser. I served that night too. I saw all the people who came to support you all. I knew a lot of them and some I had never met before. They all had the same smile. They knew you. They knew Him. I was there. I almost felt guilty about it, though, because I thought, *How can I put that pressure (albeit indirectly) on a little boy and his family for bringing me back to the church? To God?* But after

---

1     These emails have been lightly edited and condensed from their original versions. Used with permission.

listening to you and Rachel and seeing how fully and completely you were with God, I just . . . let it go.

I introduced Trey to my kids by photo at first, but they met him at the church. My oldest helped in the kids' room and would regale me with tales of Trey and how he was just a "crazy kid running all over the place" (her words. LOL). And we talked about how great it was to see him with so much energy. He was always prayed for over our meals and at bedtime. And when I would read your blog, they would see when it was a bad day for Trey because I am a sap and you can read my emotions all over my face. My extended family would get all the updates, and I would tell anyone who would listen how this little boy brought me back. Woke me up. For that, I am so thankful.

I saw your posts on Facebook, and my gosh how you made me laugh sometimes. I could not figure out how in the world you could still have such a sense of humor during this journey. Then I realized that maybe that is how God was getting to me. I understood your humor, and if I chose to make a comment or send a message . . . well, you got mine. You spoke like a real person. You are not "that kind of pastor." Thank God for that, Jay! Rachel, you have taught me so many things that I cannot begin to thank you. You are strong; you are funny and carry a sense of wisdom about you. That may sound odd, but I admire you so much. Another thing I think that made me so at ease with you is, of all things, your tattoos. You and Jay are about as down-to-earth and approachable as two people can be. You are great parents, good people. You all brought me back. Not just Trey. I cannot tell you how proud (maybe not the right word) and happy I was to see you both on your anniversary night out. I was feeling very protective of you both there at the bar and kept giving my patrons the stink eye to keep their P's and Q's about them while you were there.

I am not going to lie; when I read that Trey's battle had ended, I lost it. I didn't see until later in the afternoon after you posted. I was at work. I had to leave. I was/am angry. I thought, *How in the world could God have used this sweet little boy to bring me back and then just take him away?* I thought for sure, I was certain, he was going to be the miracle. I knew it wouldn't be an easy road, but I thought surely that was how it would be. Now, weeks after, I think, *You dummy! You caused this turn; you expected the miracle, and so you with your expectations caused this to happen.* I know this is foolish because God does what He does. But the thought has crossed my mind. As a full-grown adult person, my logical brain tells me that there is nothing I could have done to change the outcome, but my heart says, *Maybe if you had made it to church more often, had prayed a little harder, had not thought the thought . . . maybe . . .*

I am still here with you both. With your family. I am working my way out of the funk I have found myself in. It is of my own doing, not yours or Trey's passing. I am still learning not to beat myself up so much, but I thank God every day for bringing you and your family into my life. It is a gift. You always say you think of me as a fourth sister (probably more along the lines of the crazy aunt that no one likes to talk about. LOL). You humble me with that thought. It makes me smile and hope that I can continue to be here for you, even if it is just to say hello and I am thinking of you. So, yes. To answer the question, I have been brought back. Seems like I have made this trip a time or two, but I am learning more each go-round, and this time, I plan on staying. If not for me, if not for God, then definitely for Trey.

Thanks,

Christina

Jay (and Rachel)—

It never ceases to amaze me the people that God randomly brings into my life. I've followed every post you've both written, have cried with almost every entry because, as most people have probably said to you, I feel as if I've walked this journey beside you by just being part of the audience, listening, weeping, cheering, and praying. I've been a practicing Catholic, but I feel so much more open and accepting of all the love God has to offer just simply by experiencing your own journey. How raw your emotions, fears, and heartache; how joyful, happy, and full of God's love. Trey has brought me so much closer to Him and simply uplifted me in ways I never imagined. I can't begin to describe to you how privileged I felt to be able to send up my prayers for Trey and all of you.

All I really want to say is thank you for your honesty. Thank you for your openness. I, along with many, many others, thank God for you.

Blessings,

Rebecca

---

It's not really your journey with Trey's illness that has profoundly impacted my life; it is your journey through his death. I didn't join you until the journey was over. It was a post shared to a Facebook site that randomly made its way to my wall: "Pray for the Mitlo family in the loss of their son." I am a pastor, and such posts always cause me to pause and think of the loss to a precious family, the pastor who is caring for people, the impact on the community of faith. Something about it made me think of my home church, and I wondered where you were serving, so I googled you. I found your blog, and I started reading about being okay. I read the power of your statements, and I think I might even have commented that if you ever found yourself doubting God's touch in the midst of all of the tough days ahead, I prayed you would find someone to share a little of their faith with you, as you had with me. Death did not win; death did not steal away a life; a graduation had occurred.

I continue to read your posts because you are inspiring me every time you or your wife share something from the heart. I know all about the stages of grief, and I know how to be present, but I am learning how to invite hope into hopelessness, to see glory even in dark moments, and to allow people to be who they are, where they are. It's the best real-life training I could have virtually.

When you tell your stories, tell them as the ever-ongoing and evolving grace of God at work in willing hearts. I truly have no idea how far you will take me, but I am looking forward to the journey.

Thank you for making room at your table for strangers like me.

Sue Engle

---

Hey Uncle Jay,

For the past few years, every ounce of me wanted to move down South after college. While part of me still feels that, now after Trey has passed, I'm not sure I could ever leave this family for any real, prolonged period of time.

See you in a few days.

— Mike *(my nephew)*

---

In the eight months of getting to know the Mitlo family, I realize there are so many others who have followed the journey you all took. Not being a part of the journey and details of his four-year struggle, I only saw Trey at church. What I saw was a child full of life, and very friendly, especially with the other children. Looking at him, I stood amazed at how, at his young age, he didn't draw attention to himself, but rather acted like any six-year-old would act. He was happy so much of the time and so full of life. Even now on Sundays, not seeing him leaves an emptiness, but also gives me a thankful heart to have had a few months of knowing him. The memory of him bringing his snacks to church for Sunday lunch showed an unselfish heart in a little boy.

This whole experience has brought home to me once again the reality of life and death. One giving joy and one giving sadness. Life is fragile as Trey was fragile in so many ways. His short life has made me realize the possibility that God can call any of us home at any time. Trey's life spoke of a precious child who was so brave and so loved by so many. His life affected me in a way that no other one has.

Thank you, Mitlo family, for the privilege of knowing all of you.

Bernice Ott *(seventy-five-year-old member of our church)*

---

About ten years ago, under the Friday night lights at Warrior Stadium, stood this man in the first couple rows of the student section. I was a junior in high school, which meant I was allowed to stand close to the beginning of the student section, and that was a big deal. I was having the time of my life cheering on the Warriors with my best friends. I looked at this man in the student section thinking to myself, *Who is this guy, and why is he standing in the beginning of the student section?* This guy started talking to all the people around me, and then he introduced himself to me. He told me his name was Jay. I started to see Jay around the school at the different sporting events.

I ran cross country and track in high school. One day after cross country practice, my friend Samantha asked if I would want to go to her house that night for a Bible study. I grew up going to church every Sunday, but I didn't know much about the Bible. Some of my friends were going to the Bible study, so I decided to go too. When I arrived at the Bible study, to my surprise, I saw Jay. Jay and another adult, Hannah, were leading the Bible study. I found out that Jay and Hannah were Young Life leaders. Bible study was a lot of fun, and I was learning about stories of Jesus I never knew about. I continued to attend the Bible study throughout the year.

That summer in June 2005, I went to Young Life camp at Rockbridge, Virginia. I can honestly say that was the best week of my life. That week at camp, I committed my life to Christ. Hallelujah! I have grown closer with the Lord throughout the years, and I know He continues to shape me and mold me to be the woman He has called me to be.

Over the years, I kept in contact with Jay through Facebook. Facebook is how I found out that Jay's son Trey was diagnosed with cancer. Throughout those four years, I came alongside the Mitlo family in prayer. I joined the "Pray for Trey" group on Facebook. Tuesday nights I was in a Bible study with some friends, so every Tuesday my Bible study would pray for Trey. When I would drive by the Penn Hills exit on the Parkway, I would pray for Trey. I started to follow Jay's blog, and I began to tell my family and friends to pray for Trey.

I haven't seen Jay in years. But I felt like I was part of Trey's journey. My heart broke for the Mitlos; I cried when they cried, and I was joyful when they were joyful (Romans 12:15). I always lifted them up in prayer. The Mitlo family is still on my prayer board today.

Trey brought me back to what this life is all about, and that's having a relationship with God. In Jay's sermon right after Trey's death, he preached about Matthew 6:33: "But seek first his kingdom and his righteousness, and all these things will be given to you as well." That's exactly what the Mitlo family did during those four years; they sought God's kingdom first. But not only did the Mitlo family seek God's kingdom first over those past four years; they did so all those years ago when Jay was obedient to what God called him to do. God called Jay to love on Penn-Trafford students and share with them who Jesus was. I still get emotional today when I think about this. If Jay was never obedient to what God called him to do, I'm not sure if I would have a relationship with our Lord and Savior.

I will forever be grateful for Jay; he was the first person to tell me about Jesus. Obedience is key to your relationship with the Lord. Obedience bears fruit, and I know that through the Mitlos' obedience, they have impacted God's kingdom. Trey's life has impacted hundreds of people for God's glory. Trey brought me back to what this life is about, a relationship with God and being obedient to what He has called you to do.

Andria McCourt

---

I met Jay, Bella, and Trey for the first time a few years ago.

The woman who had organized a meal schedule for the Mitlos asked me if I could sign up for a day to take a meal to the family. I remember pulling up to the Mitlo home. Jay was outside, and I introduced myself and we went inside to put away the containers of food. Bella met me at the front door and asked me if I wanted a tour of the downstairs. Jay smiled and shrugged, and off I went. Bella took me into the living room, and Trey was sitting in front of the TV (fully clothed, which I would discover later on was not the norm for Trey). Bella pointed at Trey and said to me, "That's Trey." When she spoke his name, Trey looked up at me for a millisecond and then immediately back to the TV.

Fast forward to more recent days, when our God's Love group decided to merge with Faith Community Church. It was one of the first services where Jay was preaching, and Rachel, Joe, Bella, and Trey were sitting in the left front pew. At one point during one of the hymns, Rachel was holding Trey (who was filled with vim and vigor that day), and they were both bouncing and swaying and singing. For another brief millisecond, Trey turned around and looked back toward the pew where I was sitting. I'm fairly sure that he was not even looking in my direction. I felt like he was surveying or scanning his surroundings, and I was caught up in that scan.

Flash forward to the last time I saw Trey. It was the Sunday before he left here to be with Jesus. He looked tired and worn out. His momma held him tightly through the service, his little head resting on her shoulder. During one of the songs, Trey lifted his head and looked back toward the congregation . . . and then put his sweet little head back on his momma's shoulder.

At Trey's viewing, I stood amid all the pictures of Trey and felt his gaze washing over all the folks who came to mourn, rejoice, laugh, and cry with the Mitlos.

When I was much younger, I practiced transcendental meditation . . . trying to truly "see" and to be at peace within and to have a joyful heart. Now when I look at all the pictures of Trey on Facebook, his sweet gaze washes over me and I feel that "peace" and feel that "joy."

Pat Lutz

www.ingramcontent.com/pod-product-compliance
Lightning Source LLC
Chambersburg PA
CBHW020240130626
46549CB00005B/1991